Librarians And Online Services

by Pauline Atherton and Roger W. Christian

Knowledge Industry Publications, Inc.
White Plains, New York

Librarians and Online Services
    by Pauline Atherton and Roger W. Christian

Library of Congress Cataloging in Publication Data

Atherton, Pauline, 1929-
    Librarians and online services.

    Bibliography: p.
    Includes index.
    1. Libraries--Automation. 2. On-line data
processing. I. Christian, Roger W., 1928-   joint
author. II. Title.
Z678.9.A83   025.3'028'54   77-25275
ISBN 0-914236-13-X

Printed in the United States of America

Copyright © 1977 by Knowledge Industry Publications, Inc., White Plains
New York. Not to be reproduced in any form without written permission
from the publisher.

CONTENTS

 i. Acknowledgements.. ii
 1. Introduction and Overview....................................... 1
 2. The Extent of Online Services in Libraries..................... 12
 3. Impact on Library Staff and Administrators.................... 17
 4. Start-up Considerations....................................... 27
 5. Financial Considerations...................................... 55
 6. Modes of Operation and Service Procedures..................... 72
 7. Marketing and Promotion....................................... 89
 8. Management and Control....................................... 101
 9. Conclusions and A Look At The Future......................... 115
Selected Bibliography... 121
Index... 123

LIST OF TABLES

4-1: Online Start-up, University of Nebraska................... 30
4-2: Online Start-up, Northwestern Univ. Library.............. 31
4-3: Checklist for Observing Events in Pre-Search
     Interview (Atherton) 51
4-4: Checklist for Observing Interpersonal Communication
     During Pre-Search Interview (Atherton)................ 53
5-1: Fee Schedule, Univ. of California, San Diego............. 65
5-2: Charge Form, Univ. of California, San Diego.............. 70
6-1: Referral Sheet, Univ. Library, State U. at Albany........ 75
6-2: Search Form, Princeton................................... 77
6-3: Stanford Libraries Computer Search Service............... 79
6-4: Search Form, UCLA.. 81
6-5: Search Form, Univ. of California, Irvine................. 83
7-1: Instructional Resources at the Univ. of Minnesota........ 95
8-1: Evaluation Form, Syracuse Univ........................... 106
8-2: The Pre-Search Interview: An Assessment of
     Success (Atherton).................................... 108
8-3: Searcher's Time Sheet.................................... 111
8-4: Accounting Information Form, UCLA........................ 112
8-5: Stanford Computer Search Services Manual................. 114

ACKNOWLEDGEMENTS

The authors acknowledge with sincere thanks the assistance of many individuals who were interviewed for this publication, or who volunteered information on their own. We also wish to express our appreciation to the following institutions for permission to use or reprint forms: the University of Nebraska; Northwestern University; the University of California, San Diego; the State University of New York at Albany; Princeton University; Stanford University; UCLA; University of California, Irvine; University of Minnesota; Syracuse University.

Pauline Atherton
Roger W. Christian

1
Introduction and Overview

WHY THIS REPORT

This report deals with how and why libraries provide online reference services to their patrons. The title is deliberately chosen to reflect the cross currents that arise when a very old institution, the library, encounters a very new service, computer-based searching of bibliographic and other references.

Online services in their current form are barely 10 years old. Although they have been rapidly adopted by certain types of libraries--primarily the industrial, medical, and academic research libraries--other types of libraries, especially public and smaller academic libraries have made little effort to introduce them. Computer searching need not take place in a library at all, since computer terminals can be located in an academic department, in the office of an individual scholar or industrial scientist, and in a lab. Hence, the way librarians react to online services, and the speed with which they are adopted, may be an important harbinger of the future of the traditional library as more exotic, electronic information services develop in the decade ahead.

This particular report addresses the following questions:

• What are the advantages of online services in the library setting?

• How widespread are these services in libraries today?

• What is their impact on library staff, administration and users?

• How do such services get inaugurated and managed?

- How do they get funded and supported?
- What are the main problems in running these services?
- What is their likely future in libraries?

NATURE OF ONLINE SERVICES

The nature of online reference services is simple to sketch. Seated at a computer terminal, the online searcher is in direct contact, via a telecommunication link, with a remotely located computer system. There, machine-readable files called data bases are stored. These data bases are essentially electronic versions of the indexing and abstracting services already familiar to librarians. Through a structured protocol established by the retrieval system and using subject descriptors, key words, and basic Boolean logic, the searcher can examine the contents of the data bases.

The two most powerful characteristics of this kind of searching are that it is interactive and heuristic. That is, the searcher is able to modify and refine the search on the spot in response to the information being recieved. When the searcher is satisfied that the instructions to the computer are resulting in the retrieval of citations that are relevant and useful, he or she commands the computer to print out the citations either immediately (online) at the searcher's terminal, or later (offline) i.e., after the searcher has concluded the session.

Fundamentally, online services are automated versions of the reference services traditionally supplied to library patrons by certain special, academic, and research libraries. A retrospective search is equivalent to the manual preparation of a bibliography. It consists of a computer-aided search for references that match the interests and requests of the library patron. These are done on demand, making use of whatever pertinent data bases exist at the time.

A current awareness, or SDI (Selective Dissemination of Information), service is designed to keep a patron attuned to the material being published in his or her particular field of interest. A more or less continuous service, SDI is roughly equivalent to periodically updating bibliographies, or to regularly scanning Library of Congress proof slips and sending them to interested individuals. Each time the computer data bases are updated, the SDI search performed earlier is repeated, and as new data bases become available, they also are searched.

Both retrospective and current awareness searches may also be conducted offline in a so-called batch mode. In this mode, individual search requests are accumulated as they come into the computer center. Then on some regular schedule, all the searches in the batch are queued and processed simultaneously in a single pass through the computer. The focus of this report, however, will be the online services.

Also beyond the scope of this book are computer-based reference services involving the search and manipulation of purely statistical data, such as those on the U.S. census tapes, and services based on the computer retrieval of full-text documents in machine-readable form, such as those in some legal data bases.

Online bibliographic reference services appeared rather suddenly on the library scene in the early 1970s, and have exhibited dramatic growth in the few years they have been available. Today, most large academic libraries and a great many special libraries already provide such services, and Martha Williams of the University of Illinois estimates there are well over 3000 subscribers, including both large and small organizations to the principal online retrieval services that offer access to collections of data bases. Williams has also estimated that more than a million online searches are conducted each year, totaling hundreds of thousands of hours of computer connect time.[1]

ADVANTAGES OF ONLINE SERVICES

Online reference services offer a number of advantages over both the offline, batch mode, computer services inaugurated in the 1960s, and over the manual searching that has long been the stock in trade of researchers and reference librarians. Among the benefits of online reference services is speed, of course. Online results are available instantly, and even the bibliographies that are printed offline usually arrive by mail within a few days. By contrast, the results from batch or manual searches characteristically are not available for a matter of weeks.

Lower cost is another important advantage of online services. For example, a retrospective search covering a four year span, that might cost $200 from a batch processing service, can be conducted online in minutes for perhaps one-tenth the cost.

---

[1] Bulletin of the American Society for Information Science, vol. 3, no. 4 (April 1977).

Another advantage is versatility. A batch search must be formulated completely in advance, and is static once formulated. By contrast, an online search can be modified immediately in the light of results being achieved. As a result, online reference services can deal with much more complex questions than are practical with a manual search or possible with a batch search.

Still another advantage of online search services is their convenience. Terminals can be located wherever there is an electrical outlet and telephone. The computers and data bases can be accessed at any time during a very wide time frame of availability. Bibliographies, tailor-made for an individual library patron, can be generated at the touch of a button; and if the computer terminal is located in the library's reference section, as it commonly is, the system can be switched on and used almost spontaneously in conjunction with other bibliographic tools in the course of routine reference activities.

As a matter of fact, online searching is so convenient that a number of libraries including those at Dartmouth and at Bell Laboratories routinely use the online system as a ready resource to answer questions received at the reference desk. A very low-cost data base, such as that of the Educational Resources Information Center (ERIC), can be a convenient means for checking a particular author's whereabouts and affiliation.

Even the technical aspects of getting the library connected to the computer are simple. About all that is required is an electrical outlet, a phone line, and a computer terminal, which is simply plugged into the wall like a kitchen appliance.

It does not follow, however, that inaugurating online reference services is a simple undertaking. On the contrary, doing it _properly_ requires a substantial amount of planning and preparation, and much of it of a nature quite foreign to the staff and administration of a typical library. In fact, for many libraries, establishing online reference services would represent a quantum leap away from existing policies and goals of service. It characteristically forces a certain amount of personnel reorganization, some new positions (which might be filled by present staff), and a permanent commitment to a new level of staff training, updating, and user education.

EFFECT AND IMPLICATIONS OF ONLINE SERVICES

Particularly in academic and public libraries, but to a large extent also in special and research libraries, the inauguration of online reference services results in a profound philosophical wrench, as several of the traditional librarian's most firmly established beliefs and attitudes must be re-examined, and in many cases abandoned.

Perhaps the best publicized of these traumas is that of coming to terms with the necessity of charging fees to library patrons who use online reference services. Not only does this fly in the face of library tradition but it raises the spectre of "elitism," meaning service only to those who can afford to pay for it.

To be sure, some librarians steadfastly cling to the position that there should be no fees charged for machine-readable searches. Resolutions to this effect have been bitterly debated at annual meetings of the American Library Association. In fact, the full membership voted at the June 1977 meeting that charging fees "is discriminatory in publicly supported institutions," even though the ALA Council had voted against the resolution in its January 1977 midwinter meeting. However, the consensus of those currently involved in providing searches seems to be that fees are necessary, if not exactly desirable.[1]

Actually, online reference services are not equally available to everyone in any case. Though there are more than 300 data bases at present, there are still a great many subjects of interest to library patrons that are not covered.

Another notion that many librarians have trouble adjusting to is the need to actively go out and promote library services in order to encourage their use.

A third is the need to give up the pretense of being able to meet all -- or even most -- of a clientele's needs from the resources of a single library. By making patrons aware of a vast store of literature much too extensive to

---

[1] "It all Boiled Down to Money," Library Journal, vol. 102, no. 6 (March 15, 1977) and "The Key Word was Access," Library Journal, vol. 102, no. 14, (August 1977).

be maintained by any given library, online reference services virtually force a significant degree of interdependence on the libraries that offer them. A surge in interlibrary loan and photocopy traffic seems to be a concomitant of online bibliographic reference services.

A fourth accompaniment of online reference services -- and another that is not universally welcomed -- is the need for more or less disciplined measurement and evaluation of the results being achieved by the library staff.

A fifth is the new or heavier emphasis on staff development and training.

A sixth is a profound change in the role played by reference librarians vis-a-vis the library patrons. Searching the literature and compiling bibliographies with the aid of a computer requires skills, study, and training that one cannot expect library patrons to master. Accordingly, the reference librarian's role changes from that of "gate keeper" of the collections to that of being an active agent or advocate of a particular library patron with a specific information need or interest. It is almost as though one had quit a job in a tourist information booth to become a north woods guide.

Changes as profound and pervasive as these do not come easily. Coupled with the necessary investment, at a time when library funds are already inadequate, and with the shifts of the library's operating infrastructure necessary to assure management control of the new program, it is small wonder that the inauguration of online reference services has a significant impact on many aspects of the library's operations.

An identifiable and apparently discrete impact, however, may set up a cascade or domino effect that results in unsuspected changes far removed from the original. Moreover, the impact can be direct or indirect, and may even trigger what market researchers call a "cross impact," meaning that the original cause for the impact can itself be impacted. For a number of reasons, then, measuring and documenting much of the impact of online services on libraries is extremely difficult. And of course, in any specific library, the impact will reflect conditions peculiar to that institution.

However hard it may be to measure and document, it is clear from the experience of hundreds of public, private, academic, and government libraries that the impact of online reference services is, for the most part, readily <u>perceived</u>, and, fortunately, at least the general thrust and <u>nature</u> of the impact is readily predicted.

Impact on Administration

More specifically, the impact on the library administration will include the necessity to budget for the full cost of providing the services, and decisions on how any expenses not recovered from the library patrons will be funded. In most cases, these decisions mean setting up billing and collection procedures, and revising established accounting systems.

The close monitoring and control of the costs associated with the new service may suggest an examination or re-examination of the cost of some other services traditionally provided by the library. Consequently, a certain amount of policy formulation and reformulation may be in order.

A modicum of new equipment is required. Certain staff reassignments and rescheduling will be imperative. Provision will have to be made for work space and supporting materials. A program to alert patrons to the availability of the new service (a program which may become a full-blown promotion and marketing compaign) must be planned and executed. Finally, some reallocation of resources will almost certainly be required.

Impact on Reference Services

There will be a major impact on reference services, of course, and in many libraries the chief impact is that the availability of online reference services makes it possible for the first time for the library to offer bibliographic search services of any kind. Be that as it may, there will inevitably be an increased work load on the staff, new forms and policies, and changes in operating procedure. Typically these include:

1) spending more time with each individual patron than has been customary, as each online search is tailored exactly to one person's interest;

2) switching in most cases to a system of advance appointments, as contrasted with spontaneously serving patrons on a walk-in basis;

3) at least for challenging searches, having the patron physically present during the session at the computer terminal.

The reference service is liable to have to rearrange at least some of its priorities and to make provision for both formal and tutorial staff training and development. Supervision and coordination may also have to be enhanced, particularly in multi-unit libraries or in institutions with several different libraries.

Another impact is the library's enhanced ability to bring sophisticated reference services to potential users that it has been unable to serve before. For instance, many academic libraries find that they can provide online reference services to graduate students, and in some cases undergraduates, who could not be accommodated previously-- at least not on an individual basis.

Impact on Other Library Services

Other library services will also be impacted. The output of an online bibliographic reference search is typically a list of citations; some, perhaps, with abstracts of the cited articles. Except for the few library patrons who may be compiling bibliographies as an end in themselves, however, most patrons are not seeking citations, per se, but the underlying information. Accordingly, at the conclusion of the online search they are in hot pursuit of full-text copies of the relevant documents cited. A library can therefore expect demand for photocopies and microforms to soar.

Not only does online searching lead to a greater volume of interlibrary loans, it also causes changes in a library's own circulation patterns. There will be heavier use--and perhaps some abuse--of collections, and possibly a need to reassess both those areas of the current collection that are in heavy demand, and those that are in little or no demand.

Another impact of online services, on both the reference and all other departments of the library, is the intensified internal competition for funds.

Impact on Library Users

The impact on the library's patrons-- and perhaps on other outsiders as well-- typically includes a refurbished image of the library, increased patronage, not only of the online reference services but of the other library services as well, and wider appreciation of, and support for, the contributions that the library makes to the community it serves.

In some ways, however, the most important impact on library patrons is the perception and acknowledgement of reference librarians as information professionals. Librarians are seen as valuable resources whose insights and expertise can not only save the library patron enormous amounts of time, but can give him ready access to information sources he never knew about. This is a refreshing improvement over the prevalent image of the librarian as a chilly humanoid whose index finger, when not pressed to her lips, is used principally to point to the card catalog or the reference table.

PROBLEMS AND PROGRESS

Despite the effectiveness and value of online services, and the rapidity with which they are gaining converts, these systems, at the present state of the art, certainly do not represent the millennium.

Take one often mentioned limitation. During an online session at the computer terminal, it is now relatively easy for a searcher to switch from one data base to another, while browsing for relevant information. However, it is not yet possible to switch quickly between a reference file and a catalog file, in order to seek the location of full-text documents underlying the retrieved citations. Both holdings information and citation data bases are currently available online, and it is already technically feasible to link the two. It seems to be only a matter of time (and economics, of course) before this is in fact done, and it will represent a major advance.

Another problem is cost. While already much lower in cost than comparable computer-based batch searching, online reference searching is still noticeably expensive. However, the associated systems costs, i.e. computer power, computer storage, and telecommunications, show every sign of continuing to drop dramatically as they have been doing for the past 25 years. But the issue of cost has a psychological dimension. Although people with a need for important and timely information have long been accustomed to paying for it in the form of books, periodicals, reports, proceedings, and the like, they are not used to paying for it at the library. Nor, except for taking in nickels and dimes as fines, are librarians used to collecting money. (There is also little experience in paying for electronic, rather than printed, dissemination of information.)

Certainly the charges for online searches seem reasonable when the potential patron's only real alternative is to manually compile, or have compiled for him, a comparable list of citations, the production of which will take days of intensive efforts instead of a few moments at the computer terminal. As the cost of online reference services continues to decline, while their acceptance and popularity spread, it seems likely that the cost bugaboo will quietly evaporate. People will become accustomed to budgeting for online services just as they do for the print materials that they need.

Another issue in provision of online services concerns the advisability of having an intermediary. Some observers are of the opinion that the current necessity for having a specially trained reference librarian act as an interpreter between the system and the library patron is a major disadvantage that is retarding the growth in the use of these systems. The feeling is that, ultimately, the library patron ought to be able to use the system directly, bringing to bear on the search his own understanding of his exact needs and his mastery of the subject matter. In response to this contention, at least one so-called "plain language system" (ROBOT)[1] has been developed and is in operation. This system accepts commands and search inquiries expressed in ordinary English language, rather than in the structured syntax peculiar to each individual data base. It seems probable that further developments along this line will be forthcoming.

Meanwhile, the popularity of online bibliographic reference services, as presently constituted, continues to mushroom, and new vendors of data bases, retrieval services, and the associated equipment, and telecommunications and channels are entering the field, further enhancing the scope of the offerings available. Online reference serv-

---

[1] Robert Landau "ROBOT: An English Language Query Facility for Use with Data Base Management and Retrieval Systems" in Information Politics: Proceedings of the ASIS Annual Meeting, 1976 (Washington, DC: American Society for Information Science, 1976).

ices are a natural and important extension of the services the library makes available to its clientele. They are definitely here to stay. They do, however, impose fundamental and far-reaching (even if predominantly positive) changes -- changes that for the most part can be anticipated and intelligently managed -- to assure maximum benefit to the library and its staff and, more importantly, to the clientele it serves.

2
The Extent of Online Services in Libraries

Nobody seems to know just how many active users of online services there are. Moreover, surprisingly little information has been published about the individuals who have patronized these services or the uses to which they have put the results. Estimating the number of using libraries is more complicated than simply adding together the number of subscribers to each of the data base vendors. In the first place, the vendors themselves tend to regard specific data about their subscriber lists as proprietary information. In the second, many -- probably most -- libraries that offer online services subscribe to the service of two or more vendors.

INSTITUTIONAL USERS

Ronald P. Quake, president of Bibliographic Retrieval Services, Inc., points out still another complication: "To get on the client lists of my worthy competitors, all an institution has to do is sign a piece of paper," he noted in an interview. "They don't have to use the system. On the other hand, the 500 or so subscribers to BRS are economically committed to use it, and they do." People in a number of libraries that subscribe to both Lockheed and SDC services readily admitted that they made much heavier use of one system than of the other, but as the neglected system represents virtually no incremental cost there is every incentive to remain a subscriber to it.

Martha Williams of the University of Illinois estimates that perhaps 400 university libraries in the U.S. are currently online, and that the heaviest users are industry, government, and academic libraries, in that order.

Her estimates are corroborated by much of what fragmentary information is available. For instance, the New York Times Information Bank revealed to the authors that NYTIB subscribers break down as follows:

          Special   46%
          Other   26
          Government   18
          Academic   10

("Other" includes a very large number of law firms)

Similarly, one source estimates that Lockheed's subscriber list breaks out roughly as 50% special and public libraries (predominantly the former), 25% government, and 25% academic. A System Development Corporation survey three years ago by Wanger et al.[1] found that the 472 cooperating managers represented organizations that were categorized as follows:

          Commercial   32.2%
          Educational   30.7
          Government   21.3
          Other   15.7

The "educational" group in this case includes not only colleges and universities, but also junior and community colleges and local, intermediate, and county school district units. "Other" includes hospitals, not-for-profit organizations, and the like.

END USERS

If the total number of institutions utilizing online services is open to conjecture (and Williams suggests that there are between 3000 and 4000, worldwide, with perhaps 90% in the U.S.), the number and nature of the end users of these services is open to sheer guesswork. Surprisingly little data appears to have been collected on the subject, and very little of this has appeared in print. The few fragments that exist are interesting, but less revealing than they might be. Nevertheless, they will have to do, until someone sees fit to make a disciplined and detailed study of the matter.

Betty Miller and David Mindel reported at the mid-year meeting of the American Society for Information Science (ASIS) in Syracuse, May 19-21, 1977 that Calspan Corp. (formerly Cornell Aeronautical Laboratory) is one of the few companies that serve outsiders as well as its own personnel with online searches. Currently, some 64% of its "outside" business is done with other libraries -- mainly small technical ones that cannot justify their own online installation. Another 21% is done with small companies, again predominantly those engaged in research and development or producing technical products. The remaining 15% is a mixed bag ranging from lawyers and teachers to a college administrator, a market researcher, and some students, including high school students working on an NSF grant.

---

[1] Wanger, Cuadra & Fishburn, *Impact of Online Retrieval Services: A Survey of Years 1974-75* (Santa Monica: SDC, 1976).

Students were clearly the dominant category of online users during the DIALIB project, during which four neighboring public libraries south of San Francisco were experimentally linked to the Lockheed stable of online data bases. While the predominance of students was predictable during the period when the service was offered free to all comers, it persisted through the subsequent phase, when patrons had to pay for the service. During that phase, patrons gave their occupations as follows (top five categories only):[1]

	San Jose	Santa Clara	San Mateo	Redwood City	Total
Grad/undergrad	21.7%	19.4%	29.6%	42.0%	27.5%
Educators	23.9	16.4	4.5	11.4	16.9
Tech/professional	13.3	15.2	6.8	9.7	12.3
Librarian	5.3	13.3	13.6	6.3	8.3
M.D./lawyer, etc.	2.7	3.6	25.0	6.8	5.7

Students also responded most heavily to the invitation to have a free search performed online during the six-month introductory period (early 1976) at the University of California, San Diego:

Undergrad students	14%) total	40%
Graduate students	26%)	
Academic staff (excluding faculty)		26
Faculty		20
Hospital interns, residents		9
Non-academic staff		5

Interestingly, the search topics selected by the undergraduate students could not be distinguished from those chosen by researchers, faculty, or graduate students in terms of sophistication or overall breadth of interest. They included such topics as "artificial intelligence," "hydrodynamic stability," and the "use of proline hydroxylase as a prognostic tool in myocardial infarct."[2]

The reason given by the undergraduate UCSD users for having an online search conducted were as follows:

---

[1] Ahlgren, Alice, Investigation of the Public Library as a Linking Agent to Major Scientific, Educational, Social and Environmental Data Bases, Two-Year Interim Report, Annex I: Evaluation Results (Palo Alto: Lockheed Information Systems, 1976).

[2] William E. Maina, "Undergraduate Use of Online Bibliographic Retrieval Services," ONLINE Magazine, April 1977.

```
        Prepare a class assignment
          (excluding independent study)  34%
        An on-going research project
          (not class-related)            21
        Explore a personal interest      12
        Independent study or honors
          thesis                         11
        No response                      22
```

Not surprisingly, the reasons for getting online searches done at the public libraries involved in the DIALIB experiment differ, but the preponderance of classroom and scholarly concerns is still much in evidence:

Reason	San Jose	Santa Clara	San Mateo	Redwood City	Total
Research paper	48.2%	30.3%	40.9%	48.3%	42.9%
Job or business	27.9	45.4	38.6	21.1	31.5
School assignment	12.4	5.5	6.8	7.4	8.7
Personal interest	3.5	4.2	4.5	5.7	4.4
Graduate degree program	3.1	4.2	2.3	6.3	4.3
Book	0.4	0.6	0.0	0.6	0.5
Research & Development	0.0	0.0	0.0	0.6	0.2

Virtually all of the DIALIB users were well educated, a characteristic that can probably be safely imputed to online users everywhere.

```
        Graduate student
          (past or present)   33.4%
        Master's degree       17.8
        College graduate      11.8
        College student        9.7
        PhD or MD              5.9
        High school student    0.3
```

The relative paucity of users with an M.A. or Ph.D (as opposed to those seeking such a degree) is interesting. It is even more interesting in light of a surprising study of the information sources used by typical bioscientists, which was reported in May, 1977.[1] If any particular group could be expected to regularly take advantage of online searching, one would certainly think that bioscientists would do so. They have been bombarded by MEDLINE and MEDLARS promotion for half a decade, they routinely use computers in their research and teaching, and they are typically well aware of bibliographic and other information sources.

---

[1] Dade T. Curtis, "Has the End User Been Forgotten?" in The Value of Information, Collected Papers of ASIS Mid-year meeting, May 19-21, Syracuse University.

Still, the scientists in the sample studied make surprisingly little use of online searching, despite ready access to it. The sample was small but characteristic: 57 men and one woman, median age 35 years, all with doctorates except two, who are doctoral candidates. They come from 18 states and five other countries, and represent 20 medical schools, seven graduate universities, three non-profit research institutes, two government labs, and an industrial research center. During the past six years, 86% of them have published at least two professional papers, and 82% have received at least one grant.

Online search facilities are available to 86% of them via their faculty status at medical or other schools. Yet 57% have never requested a computer search, either online or batch. Only one individual uses interactive services for current awareness searching, while five rely on them for retrospective searches. To the extent that these findings can be extrapolated to the community of campus bioscientists at large, it seems safe to suggest that the total potential market for online services is far from being adequately penetrated.

3
Impact on Library Staff and Administrators

Online bibliographic search services characteristically have a substantive impact on the reference department of the libraries that institute them. This is particularly true for academic and public libraries, which traditionally have not provided personalized services for their patrons. To them, online data bases have brought an entirely new role. At special libraries, which are accustomed to conducting personalized bibliographic searches, the availability of online data bases has drastically reduced the drudgery and tedium involved, while making the process much faster and more comprehensive. For nearly all libraries, however, the availability of online services has shifted what might be called the "philosophy" of research libraries in very perceptible ways.

Traditionally, reference librarians have compiled specialized bibliographies -- normally useful to an entire group of students, scholars, or researchers. They have also typically referred library patrons to sources of information, such as the card catalog and the indexing and abstracting services in print form. Less commonly, they may have performed bibliographic research in pursuit of answers to specific questions raised by patrons. That is, they functioned as surrogates in digging out the specific information that a patron needed, although they rarely spent much time working on the patron's problem.

This entire modus operandi changes with the introduction of online bibliographic reference services. Armed with the equipment, knowledge and search aids that provide access to machine-readable data bases stored in a remote computer, reference librarians can now quickly compile bibliographies of recent journal articles that are custom tailored to the interests of a single library patron. Moreover, the product or output of an online literature search is not in itself an "answer" -- the end information that the library patron is seeking. Instead, it is a list of citations -- with or without abstracts -- that appear to be relevant to his needs.

In short, with online services the reference librarian's role shifts from one of being a sort of archivist-in-residence to that of an information specialist. Whereas the archivist has extensive knowledge of the library's inventory and working familiarity with the printed indexing services, the specialist is actively involved in retrieving and disseminating bibliographic information, individually compiled and packaged for one specific patron.

A related impact of online services is that both the nature of the librarian's activities in this connection and the sheer popularity of the services tend to add to the work load of the reference librarians. A number of studies have been made to determine the average time spent on a "typical" online bibliographical search. While the range of absolute values is so broad as to be almost meaningless--unless the studies are applied to a single institution--it appears to be a rough rule of thumb that a skilled and experienced information librarian must devote about twice as much time with the library patron before and after the search, as he or she does in conducting the search at the computer terminal. Charlotte Sakai of the San Jose Public Library observed that for every minute on-line, an operator spends three minutes offline.

The System Development Corp. survey of 546 online installations, including those serving government, educational, commercial, and other patrons, indicates that the median time required for a complete online search is between 40 and 50 minutes.[1] This time is divided roughly in thirds, devoted to pre-search negotiations, actual time at the terminal, and post-search activities. In commercial organizations however, many searchers spend more than an hour in post-search work; evaluating, reorganizing, packaging, and in many cases adding explanatory notes, summaries or commentaries to the results, before submitting them to the library patron.

Exacerbating the added work load on the reference librarians is the fact that online services, once instituted, tend to attract additional patronage as they gain popularity. Moreover, as patrons prefer online searches to manual ones, the total demand for such services tends to increase the longer they are available. As a rather extreme instance, the SDC survey uncovered one organization that experienced a 10-fold increase in the number of online search requests

---

[1] Wanger et al., op. cit.

over a 12-month period. At Bell Laboratories, where only 25% of all literature searches were conducted online in 1973, nearly all searches undertaken in 1975 were done by machine -- and there were about twice as many searches. Online usage tripled again in 1976, and that total, in turn, was surpassed in the first seven months of 1977. Equally impressive was the 200% increase in online search volume between July and December 1976 at Oregon State University, according to librarian Kris Brooks.

Another measure of increased work load was recorded at the Redwood City public library in California, where the inauguration of online searching services increased the professional work load by about 20 hours per week.

Other aspects of the added burden placed on reference librarians by online services include the fact that in many cases the availability of online services has enabled a number of libraries to offer bibliographic reference services for the first time. Another is that once a list of citations or abstracts has been retrieved, the reference librarians are normally called upon to assist the patrons in acquiring full-text copies of at least some of the referenced material. Libraries providing these services characteristically report substantial increases in the volume of photocopying and fiche copying, and in the volume of interlibrary loans. Among the specific measured instances of this are the statistics presented by Jean Martin of Russell Research Center of the U.S. Department of Agriculture in Athens, GA, who found that "the higher volume of interlibrary loan requests" in 1976 "correlated with requests for literature searches."[1] At the Murray Hill, NJ library of Bell Labs, interlibrary loans jumped 67% between 1974 and 1975 as online searching grew.[2] In addition, circulation of materials in a library's own collections also rises.

A dramatic example of one of these ancillary impacts is the case of the library which following the introduction of free searches of the ERIC data base noted a 200%

---

[1] Martin, Jean K., "Impact of Computer-Based Literature Searching on Interlibrary Loan Activity," Proceedings of the ASIS Annual Meeting, 1977 (White Plains, NY: Knowledge Industry Publications, 1977).

[2] Hawkins, Donald, "Impact on On-Line Systems on Literature Searching Service" at 10th Middle Atlantic Regional Meeting, (Philadelphia: American Chemical Society, 1976).

increase in the volume of copying of related fiche materials from the library's report collection. While this situation is extreme, it is characteristic for libraries to experience a significant increase in the level of copying of cited materials associated with online searching.

As the volume of interlibrary loans also increases-- sometimes rather dramatically-- with the introduction of online services, some libraries have tried to streamline their interlibrary loan procedures, so that the full-text documents that have to be borrowed are made available to the user rapidly, in keeping with the fast turnaround times associated with computer searching.

As a matter of fact, some library directors have complained that the speed and comprehensiveness of online literature searching tends to escalate user expectations of the library as a whole to sometimes unrealistic levels. Users seem to think that the library is automated in everything, and they are very demanding about getting faster photocopies, printed journals, and interlibrary loans so that they can take immediate advantage of the bibliographic citations produced by the computer search.

The intensification of interlibrary loan activity is likely to produce another indirect impact in the next few years. Already, some libraries that are heavy net lenders in interlibrary loan networks have instituted fees or other charges to help them recover some of the expense of this activity and to encourage borrowers to disperse their requests more widely. Cornell and the University of Toronto are examples.

While most librarians seem to rely heavily on interlibrary loans for obtaining materials they do not have in their own collections, they also make changes in their acquisition programs. About 28% of the library managers surveyed by Wanger et al. reported such adjustments. Most of them had to increase journal subscriptions, and a few also had to adjust their collection of monographs. A number of libraries have also chosen to buy microform collections of reports, and to change their collection development procedures to relate them more closely to the content of the data bases that they were using.

Heavier use of the library's collections has also led, unfortunately, to heavier abuses. All too often, unscrupulous patrons, armed with long lists of references from their computer search, invade the library shelves and razor out relevant articles.[1] Even in the absence of this sort of atrocity, the ease with which end users can now obtain pertinent citations has commonly increased the work load on the circulation staff.

The introduction of computer-based literature searching also affects the non-professional library staff. For example, those who man the reference desk may require better instruction in the use of printed indexes, so that, in handling inquiries, they can identify the persons who could benefit most from online services, while referring others to printed sources. The added work load for the non-professional staff also includes new clerical, recordkeeping, and other duties, such as forwarding results to the patrons. At the same time there is more work in the purchasing and accounting departments, as libraries take on the tasks of ordering supplies and equipment associated with online searching, of monitoring their online usage, and of passing along all or part of the charges to users.

Partly offsetting the additional work loads imposed, online systems greatly increase the productivity of reference librarians. Evidence for this proposition comes from the SDC survey in which more than three out of four of 472 managers and 801 librarians and information specialists agreed that online services "greatly increased" the productivity of the professional staff.[2]

Another major impact of the introduction of online search services is the increased professionalism of the staff and the enhanced self image of the reference librarians. In fact, an entirely new type of librarian is emerging: professionals who specialize in providing information services through machine-readable data bases. Their titles range from "information specialist" used at Syracuse University, to the straightforward "data services librarian" used at the University of Kentucky, and on to "search consultant" used at Oregon State. These specialists, who will be referred to here as information services librarians, concentrate on knowing what data bases exist, what their contents are, how they are organized and indexed, where they are located, and how best and most efficiently to take maximum advantage of them.

These new professionals are skilled at helping library patrons isolate and articulate their information needs, at

---

[1] As happened at the UCLA Biomedical Library.

[2] Wanger et al. op. cit.

selecting and evaluating data bases, at developing and refining effective search strategies, and in helping their clientele get the maximum benefit from online searching. They are familiar with various indexing techniques and the use of controlled vocabularies and, of course, are fully familiar with available conventional bibliographic search tools and full-text resources.

The enhanced image of librarians, both in their own eyes and in the eyes of their users, stems from a number of factors. Because the computer has taken much of the tedium out of literature searching, the librarian has more opportunities for rewarding face-to-face relationships with library patrons. There is also the recognition that online systems make it possible for librarians to provide substantially better service to their patrons and to demonstrate expertise in the process--both factors that make the job more rewarding.

This increased self esteem and feeling of professionalism has been expressed in a number of ways. One active information services librarian said in an interview: "During the pre-search interview I really feel like an analyst who needs to get a very clear understanding of the search request. Then I know and the user knows that all is in good hands." Another commented, "I am being perceived as a professional, not just a library clerk. The user knows he is dealing with someone very much like a doctor who can diagnose his needs and respond to them professionally and effectively." Phyllis Jaynes, online services coordinator at the Feldberg Library at Dartmouth, points out that people visiting the Tuck Business and Sayer Engineering Schools she serves "often make a beeline for the library, now," which was hardly considered a campus highlight before the computer terminal was installed.

Other departments of the library besides reference may benefit from this new-found prestige. Heightened user interest and appreciation may be translated into increased usage of library services generally.

Another major impact that online services have on the reference department is the requirement for new policies and procedures. Most dramatically, the institution of online search services nearly always carries with it the requirement to charge fees to patrons. This in turn, especially in academic libraries, commonly forces some sort of segmentation of users.

For example, academic libraries typically divide their online patrons into three categories:

• Faculty members are charged a fee, normally set so that the institution can recover the direct, incremental costs of providing online services: computer connect time, communications costs, and printing costs;

• Graduate students often are afforded access to online searches at a discount, with the institution absorbing a portion of these direct costs;

• Off campuses users -- such as local businesses -- are charged the full, direct cost of providing online searches plus a surcharge, directed at recapturing the overhead and true staff costs associated with conducting the search.

For example, Oregon State University insists that each member of the campus community pay the direct costs of online searches. Academic users from other colleges pay direct costs plus a $5.00 charge for staff time. Non-academic users pay the direct costs plus a surcharge of $15 per hour of library staff time. (Fee policies are dealt with more fully in chapter 5.)

Still others, such as the University of Pennsylvania and Stanford University, elect to segment online searches into "standard" and "special," or custom searches. Standard searches, normally restricted to relatively simple searches against a single data base, with limitations on the number of citations permitted, are provided at a relatively low cost. More complex searches are provided on a custom basis, with charges reflecting both the direct, incremental costs, and, in some cases, at least partial recovery of staff and overhead costs.

Online services also impose the need for more active user education. The chronic problem of communication between the library patron and the reference librarian is often intensified when the user must be brought to think in terms of specific key words and controlled vocabularies. In addition, many library users exhibit considerable curiosity about computer-based reference systems themselves, and in the characteristics and content of the various data bases. Another common problem is that of disabusing first time users of unrealistic expectations.

Similarly, the advent of online systems imposes the necessity for informing patrons of their existence. Often, this means aggressive promotion and marketing--activities that are traditionally foreign to reference librarians. Even though an aggressive promotional compaign may have been mounted, complete with brochures, slide shows, posters, demonstrations, and the like, the most pivotal role still falls to the information services librarian, who is in regular face-to-face contact with interested patrons. "No other form of promotion is as convincing as a well satisfied customer," said Ellen Pearson at the University of Guelph in Ontario.

Staff training and orientation must also precede, accompany, and follow the introduction of online search services. Not only must reference librarians undergo such training initially, but they must subsequently provide it to other members of the staff, while themselves staying abreast of developments in this highly dynamic field. Online services also impose increased demands on the supervision of the reference department, on the coordination of online searching efforts in multi-unit institutions, and on cooperation and liaison with other organizations -- including, of course, suppliers of the equipment, services, and supplies for online searching.

One relatively common change instituted by libraries in conjunction with providing online services is the practice of handling search requests on an appointment basis.[1] Such appointments are scheduled not only for private, pre-search interviews and strategy sessions, but sometimes for post-search debriefings, during which the search specialist reviews the retrieved citations and/or abstracts and helps the patron assess their relevance.

During these sessions the librarian also apprises the patron of what full-text materials are available in that library or elsewhere, and integrates the computer output with the other library resources. For example, it might be appropriate to pursue the topic further back in time through printed indexing and abstracting media, which might cover older material than that available online. Similarly, arrangements can be made during the interview to acquire full-text copies of the more important cited material, perhaps via photocopy or interlibrary loan.

Once instituted in connection with online services, the practice of scheduling specific appointments tends to be extended to other aspects of the reference department's activities, including bibliographic consulting services, tutorials, demonstrations, and the like.

---

[1] The University of Toronto is one of many examples.

The practice of working on an appointment basis enables the library staff to discipline and schedule its own activities and to create a business-like atmosphere that adds to their feeling and image of professionalism. As a matter of fact, the prestige accorded information services librarians has the potential of triggering jealousies within the reference department staff. Those not involved in online searches may perceive these specialists as a kind of elite, exclusive group.

Probably the most important impact that online search services have on the reference department, however, is that of greatly expanding its ability to serve. We have already alluded to the phenomenon of online services enabling many libraries to inaugurate literature search services where none existed before, or to extend greatly the scope of such services.

Moreover, online systems dramatically expand the body of literature to which the reference librarian has convenient access. E.g., online systems offer ready access to the traditionally elusive report literature, particularly through data bases generated by the National Technical Information Service (NTIS), ERIC, the Smithsonian Institution, and the Defense Documentation Center.

The ability to provide new and better services to a wider clientele is not only gratifying to the library professional but satisfying to the library's patrons. The overall result is to greatly enhance the utility, value, and prestige of the library within the community it serves.

IMPACT ON LIBRARY ADMINISTRATORS

Many of the impacts of online services discussed in this chapter become matters to be decided by the library administrator. This is particularly true because online systems have strong economic ramifications, calling for executive policy decisions.

The question of charging or not charging end users is the best example. Almost no library these days has discretionary funds to pour into computer-based retrieval, nor are government or foundation grants readily available for this purpose. Thus, library administrators have the tough choice of cutting services in some other area, or of instituting fees for online users.

What's more, the economic decisions do not end with charging or not charging. As noted earlier, installation of online retrieval often highlights questions about the allocation of the library's acquisition budget, the adequacy of its staff training and retraining expenditures, and the need to actively promote services to users. Unless the administrator addresses these problems directly, the danger is that online services will either languish for lack of support, or will force far-reaching changes in library operations without a conscious decision that such changes are necessary or desirable.

The real point is that libraries cannot "back into" online services, nor can administrators delegate the important decisions to lower level supervisors. Realizing the obvious benefits of these systems requires the active involvement of the head of the library in planning, budgeting, and managing. These activities will be the subject of extended discussion in the chapters to come.

4
Start-up Considerations

In this era of escalating costs and increasing competition for the scarce funds available, libraries, particularly academic and public libraries, have often found it difficult to win approval and money for new projects and services. Provision of online bibliographic retrieval systems is subject to these pressures, and in addition faces several other obstacles. Among them is the fact that the need for online services is not readily recognized and accepted by some administrators, particularly in the light of competition for scarce funds. Moreover, while the relatively substantial cost of providing such services is highly visible, the cost of not providing them is not. Besides, the cost effectiveness of such services is not easily demonstrated.

THE PRELIMINARY PROPOSAL AND STUDY

Once library officials perceive the desirability of offering such services, it behooves them to carefully document the need for and benefits of, such services. Someone must delineate the scope and prospects of such services at the particular library, or within the particular organization involved; prepare estimates of the volume and costs that can be realistically anticipated; estimate both the positive and the negative impacts that such services are likely to have on the library and the community it serves; and in general, demonstrate that the idea has been carefully investigated and analyzed. The result should be a persuasive, written proposal for top management consideration.

One acceptable approach, which has the added merit of increasing library staff's interest in, and commitment to, online reference services, is for the library director to appoint a study group, or at least an individual, to investigate existing online systems and services in comparable libraries.[1] While the output of such a study is commonly an extensive memorandum or report to the library director, it could just as well take the form -- or perhaps the additional form -- of an oral report to some administrative meeting of appropriate library officials and staff.

Either way, such a report would probably include a general description of the current state of the art and trends in the field, perhaps some discussion of its historical development and potential, and commentary specific to the library involved on such matters as these:

. The implications and applicability of lessons learned at other institutions;

. The kinds of services and modes of operation that seem most appropriate to the clientele serviced by this library;

. The service vendors and specific data bases that are most likely to appeal to the library's clientele, and that most closely parallel its collections and the interests of the population it serves;

. The competitive factors to be considered if more than one potential vendor offers appropriate data bases and services;

. The impact that a decision to provide such services might have on the staff, work load, responsibilities -- particularly at the reference desk -- schedules, attitudes, and morale of the library staff;

. The possible need to bolster document delivery services in some way;

. The adaptability of key members of the current staff to training in the provision of online services;

. Some notion of the nature, locations, and volume of demand for such services among the library's clientele;

. Some informed conjecture about the likely cost effectiveness of such services;

. At least a rough forecast of the initial costs that would be involved.

---

[1] The University of Rochester (NY) followed this plan.

Such costs vary considerably, as witness estimates drawn up in proposals prepared for the University of Nebraska, in Lincoln, and for Northwestern University. (Tables IV-1 and IV-2) The Lincoln, Nebraska proposal calls for a single teletype-compatible terminal to be moved as needed between two libraries on the campus, and affording access only to the family of data bases offered by Lockheed Information System. The Northwestern University proposal envisions access to the data bases covered by System Development Corporation as well as by Lockheed (and, subsequently, to the New York Times Information Bank) via a relatively sophisticated video terminal in each of two library facilities.

For such an internal report to the library director to be used as the basis for a formal proposal, it would have to be elaborated upon. Supporting data should include an estimate of the number of searches that are likely to be generated on such a system during the first year; estimates of the necessary professional and support staff required to provide the forecast level of service; a tentative budget; an outline of plans for promoting and marketing the service; a plan for training the staff; a proposed organization; plans for recovering at least some of the costs of providing the search service; and a firm recommendation for action.

Normally, such proposals also include a timetable for implementing the services, if the proposals are approved. It is also a good idea for the library director to have at least a mental timetable for reassessing the situation, and possibly preparing a second and stronger proposal, in the event the initial one is rejected.

Such administrative considerations as the detailed financial and promotional aspects of providing online services, and establishing service procedure and administrative controls, are dealt with in some detail in subsequent chapters. In addition to these, however, library administrators bent on successfully inaugurating online bibliographic reference services must give intensive attention to at least six other key elements:

- Establishing the mission of the service

- Market analysis

- Resource analysis and selection

- Organization

TABLE 4-1: ONLINE START-UP

UNIVERSITY OF NEBRASKA - LINCOLN LIBRARIES

1. Start-up Costs (January 1-June 30, 1976)

Texas Instruments 735 portable printer terminal	$ 720
Training by Lockheed personnel (est.)	900
Supplies (paper, etc.)	100
Printing of Service Brochures and forms	100
Communications during start-up	100
User manuals	20
Computer time for training additional operators	300
Total start-up costs:	$2,240

2. Continuing Costs (yr)

Terminal $120/mo.	$1,440
Supplies and maintenance	250
Yearly Cost	$1,690

TABLE 4-2: ONLINE START-UP

NORTHWESTERN UNIVERSITY LIBRARY
COMPUTER ASSISTED INFORMATION SERVICES

Estimated Costs for 1975-76

   Training (one-time costs)

      Lockheed and SDC training seminars
      (Fees and transportation to Palo Alto, CA $1,000.
      for 2 seminars for 2 people)

      Staff training for 12 staff members
      $45 - Average cost per hour of
            computer time
      $10 - TYMSHARE cost per hour
      $55 - Total cost per hour

      12 staff members x 2 hours/staff
      members x $55/hour $1,320.

   Equipment costs

      Telephone line in Reference Department $ 50. yr.
      Telephone line in Technological -
        Institute Library $ 50. yr.
      Terminal costs
        2 terminals x $140. month rental
        x 12 months/year $3,360. yr.

        Subtotal $5,780.

Staff and professional time costs

   Professional time

      3,500 searches/year x 1/2 hr./search
      x $6.00/hour $10,500. yr.

   Staff time

      3,500 searches/year x $.64/search $ 2,240. yr.

      Total $18,520.

- Providing physical facilities
- Personal selection and training

ESTABLISHING THE MISSION

Establishing a credible and achievable mission for online services at a particular library may be more complex than it might seem at first blush. It is easy to make a ringing statement about bridging the gap between the ever-increasing needs for bibliographic information to support teaching, research, and the like, and the exponential rise -- almost the explosion -- in the volume of pertinent literature. But such a pronouncement may not be enough; and in fact it <u>should</u> not be enough.

A serious statement of mission should address itself to such matters as just who will be served, and in what order of priority. The parent organization typically makes this abundantly clear to corporate and other special libraries, most of which will not do online searches for outsiders. Thus, the Charles River Associates library in Cambridge accommodates only staff members of that consulting firm. However, the issue of who will be served can generate considerable discussion in an academic or public library -- particularly where the imposition of user fees represents a distinct innovation.

Many academic libraries -- Stanford and Northwestern among them -- establish a policy of serving only the institution's faculty, staff and students. Others, including the University of California will also serve faculties, scholars and students of other institutions, often on a time-available basis. Still others, like Darthmouth, agree to accommodate requests from commercial organizations. Some tax-supported institutions such as the University of Nebraska restrict their clientele to businesses within the host state or community.

The statement of mission should also specify whether the online reference services to be provided will be restricted to retrospective searches, current awareness or SDI searches, or both.

The mode of operation, at least initially, should also be spelled out. Will the reference desk or circulation department of the library function only as a well informed referral node, sending interested patrons to other libraries that are equipped to actually conduct online searches? Or will the library function as an intermediary, offering patrons professional help in compiling interest profiles or discrete search statements and then, on the patron's behalf, getting the online searches performed at an affiliated institution with appropriate facilities? Or finally, will the library staff itself provide personalized computer-based search services at its own facilities.

Another aspect of establishing the mission for online services is to set some specific, and ideally, measurable goals and objectives of service. Chief among these in some libraries, of course, will be simply establishing, for the first time, literature searching services of any kind. Another goal might be to serve a greater number of users. A third might be to improve services through access to additional sources of information, or faster turn around time, or greater precision in the citations retrieved. A related goal might be greater user satisfaction as a result of the speed, versatility, comprehensiveness, convenience, and other benefits of online searching.

Internal objectives might include greater staff productivity, or a reduction in the staff time needed for literature searching, or perhaps an absolute reduction in reference staff. Other valid objectives might include cost effectiveness of the literature searching services, and perhaps more intensive use of the library's collections.

Another aspect of establishing the mission of the online services is to come to terms with the issue of cost recovery. Some libraries, particularly those within research-oriented corporations, have no cost recovery goals. They simply absorb the full cost of online search services within the unit's budget. Others, including Xerox, Bell Labs, and Exxon, transfer all or portions of the cost to the budgets of the company departments or specific projects making the search requests.

Most academic and the few public libraries that offer online search services, however, have felt compelled to recover at least the identifiable, direct cost of providing a computer-based search. This includes the computer connect time, the communications cost, and the cost of offline printing of the retrieved citations. A few libraries endeavor to recover all their costs, including professional and staff time and general overhead; especially with respect to searches performed for outsiders -- those not immediately connected with the sponsoring institution.

It is also conceivable that the library may establish the goal of making a profit. Currently, this is seldom done, but it does occur in situations where, for example, a strong academic library prices its online services to outside commercial organizations at a level that will yield a profit sufficient to permit the library to offer online search services to students at a significant discount. UCLA is one case.

MARKET ANALYSIS

A second major element to be considered during the start-up phase is that of market analysis. That is, just what user groups within the clientele normally served by the library have an articulated or potential use for online services, and which data bases have the most to offer them? Each identifiable user group, or potential user group, within the community served should be described in terms of its size, specific location or locations, and other pertinent characteristics, including particularly, its ability to pay. In an academic community, these resources might consist of department budgets, grants, contracts, and research funds and the like. Patrons of a public library might have to rely on personal funds, reimbursement from an employer, or money from fellowships and grants.

To the extent possible, the need of each identified potential user group for bibliographic services should be quantified, and from this some estimate should be made of the demand on the part of each group for online search services. Ideally, the magnitude of the demand for each specific data base should be estimated. As might be expected, public libraries find the demand for online bibliographic reference services more elastic than do academic libraries. However, both find it highly sensitive to price, particularly when fees are instituted after an initial period of free service.

This phenomenon, and other intangibles such as the novelty appeal of newly instituted online services, the countervailing reluctance of many people to try anything new, and the resistance of traditionalists to the whole notion of paying for any kind of library service, must be taken into account in analyzing the potential market for online services, and in forecasting levels of demand.

With these data in hand, the library is prepared to select the user community, or communities, that it will serve initially. Often, another strategic decision presents itself at this time. The relative attraction of serving a single, high-potential user group, at relatively low cost with one or two data bases, must be weighted against the lure of offering a wide spectrum of data bases, at higher risk, in the hopes of appealling to a larger number of users and user groups. Market segmentation and analysis may help provide some answers (see Chapter 7).

RESOURCE ANALYSIS AND SELECTION

The third major start-up activity is resource analysis and selection. As of this writing, libraries have little real choice in the matter of who will supply telecommunication services associated with online bibliographic searches. However, they can all choose from among at least three nationwide retrieval system vendors of multiple data bases, and a growing number of organizations that offer access to only one or a few data bases. In addition, each library must evaluate individual data bases in light of its own clientele and its own collections.

The Major Vendors

While a number of information centers and commercial organizations offer online retrieval services on a more or less localized basis, the three vendors of online retrieval services are Lockheed Information Systems, of Palo Alto, CA, System Development Corporation, of Santa Monica, CA, and a relative newcomer, Bibliographic Retrieval Services, based in Schenectady, NY. BRS began operations in January 1977, with particular emphasis on serving the academic community.

The costs of acquiring, processing, and updating machine-readable data bases, and in providing online retrieval services, do not vary greatly from one vendor to the next. In a competitive market, their prices do not vary that much either. Hence, the evaluation and selection of a retrieval service vendor should turn on an assessment of the relative match between that vendor's offerings, services, and modus operandi on the one hand, and the needs and desires of the library on the other.

The hingepin question, of course, is whether or not a vendor offers the particular data base or mix of data bases that will meet the needs of the user groups that the library intends to serve. While online access to several of the more popular data bases can be had through any of the principal vendors, other important files are uniquely available only from one.

Among the other factors to be taken into account when evaluating vendors of online retrieval services are the vendor's reputation and performance record, its reliability, speed of response, and the level of accessibility, cooperation, and support available from the vendor's specialists.

Among the technical features of a retrieval service to be considered are:

. Availability of natural language commands;

. Ease of logging in and logging off;

. Type of search available -- author, title, key word, organization name or source, etc.;

. Speed and cost of communications options; (300 or 1200 baud);

. Ease of access to search free text in record:

. Degree of logic offered -- e.g., to what extent a key word may be searched in a certain context or in relation to other terms;

. Ability to store a search for future use (as in SDI profiles);

. Times that the service is available; printing/display options.

Still another key consideration in evaluating data base vendors is the package of support services offered to users. These commonly include a limited number of free demonstrations, formal training courses and workshops for library personnel, and instruction manuals. In addition, vendors usually provide guidebooks to assist searchers in preparing SDI profiles and retrospective search strategies and some sort of newsletter designed to keep users informed about search tips and short cuts, changes in indexing practices, the availability of new data bases or new searchable data elements, and suggestions on how best to take advantage of the peculiarities of the particular system or data base.

Printed search aids such as dictionaries, thesauri and vocabulary lists, and handy reminder cards summarizing important procedures and commands are also commonly provided. So is a telephone "hotline," with which searchers can request immediate help with any equipment or search problem encountered in the course of an ongoing search.

Costs and Features

All of these are important considerations in choosing which vendors to use, but there is one more: comparative costs. The cost of a retrieval service is not the most important criterion in selecting one, but it is a long way from being an incidental matter. While prices on the average may not differ greatly, it is not unusual to discover that particular search features make it measurably cheaper to search data base X on system A, whereas system B is much the better and cheaper way to search data base Y. Accordingly, the person responsible for evaluating and selecting retrieval services must get familiar with the various fee structures and the basis for the charges associated with each candidate.

Integral to the selection of an online service is an analysis of the uses to which the service will be put. The library must ask itself whether its patrons will be primarily interested in current awareness searching, with SDI profiles being maintained for periodic searching, or in retrospective searches, e.g., to compile detailed bibliographies, answer specific questions, or identify research trends that are of concern. A related question is whether the patrons will want to take advantage of full-text document delivery, as offered in the NTIS data base, or in that of Current Contents from the Institute for Scientific Information of Philadelphia. In these cases, once having identified a relevant citation, the user can instruct the computer to transmit a request for the document itself.

Selecting Data Bases

Evaluating and selecting the specific data bases, online access to which would be most meaningful to the library's clientele, involves considering another "laundry list" of important variables. Among the chief concerns are the scope, content, and currency of the data bases themselves. Depending on the source documents utilized, some data bases are discipline-oriented (Psychological Abstracts), others are problem-oriented (ENVIRON), still others are mission-oriented (AGRICOLA), and a number of them include various combinations of these categories.

The type of source material covered may include not only articles from learned journals, but books, government reports, monographs, theses, newspaper and magazine articles, patents, and in the case of the Smithsonian Science Information Exchange, statements of the current status of ongoing research projects. A separate question is whether the source material is covered at the primary level or only at the secondary level, that is, via an indexing and abstracting service.

Another factor is the time span and timeliness of the coverage. Where clientele interest is high, data base publishers and vendors are inclined to broaden the data base's coverage by adding older, as well as newer, material. Where this has not been done, comprehensive retrospective literature searches may have to overflow from the online search to manual investigation of older literature in the more traditional print media.

The timeliness of the material in a particular data base may reflect an unconscionable lag between the time a journal article or report appears in print, and the time when its citation data finds its way into the computer memory. At the other extreme, some material may be available in machine-readable form *before* it appears in print. This could be the case where, as is increasingly common, a computer tape is used to produce the hard copy journal.

The completeness of the data base's coverage might also be questioned in certain circumstances. The fact that a particular journal is listed as being "covered" by a data base publisher or vendor does not necessarily mean that every issue of the journal is covered, nor that each issue is covered in its entirety.

The indexing and coding practices used to generate the data base constitute another subject of inquiry. Dependence on a controlled thesaurus of hierarchical vocabulary terms has important implications for the utility of the data base and for the search strategies that are brought to bear upon it. The number and kinds of access points, and the specific data elements that can be used as searchable and printable fields, are other important considerations. Does the data base include abstracts, or citations only? If abstracts are included, can they be searched as well as displayed? Can they be printed?

Another factor worth considering is the degree of overlap with other data bases that might be accessed, and the general consonance of the data base, not only with the anticipated concerns and interests of the library's clientele, but with the library's own collections. For the most part, patrons are in hot pursuit not of citations but of documents. Hence, a data base strongly oriented to subjects and materials only meagerly represented in the library's resources can generate a great deal of turbulence with respect to acquisition, collection development, and interlibrary borrowing.

The relationship between the data base and the corresponding printed index should also be investigated. While there may be a one-to-one correspondence between the two media, the machine-readable data base could also be merely a subset of the hard copy version, or conversely, more inclusive or more accessible than the counterpart printed index.

Other matters worth probing are what vocabulary aids or search aids might be available online to facilitate use of the data base, the total number of citations included, and the rate and frequency with which the data base was being updated. Finally, one should weigh the cost of searching the data base and of printing out a reasonable number of retrieved citations compared with the cost of manually searching that service.

ORGANIZATION OF SERVICE AND STAFF

The fourth matter to be deliberated and decided during the start up phase of a program to inaugurate online search services is that of organizing and locating the service. While not all libraries will be in a position to seriously consider more than one option, those that are should carefully weigh the feasibility and relative merits of each possibility. For example, the library could choose to provide all online services from a single, centralized location. MIT does this -- interestingly, after several years of using dispersed search locations. Alternatively, a given library may elect to follow the lead of the University of California at Berkeley, and conduct searches from two or more decentralized locations, each of which might specialize in providing access to a particular kind of data base (medical here, social sciences there, hard sciences somewhere else, etc.). Another possibility is to conduct online services from the central headquarters facility, while using satellite locations to screen and refer patrons.

Some libraries in peculiar circumstances might even want to consider other options, such as having information service librarians go to particular patrons and negotiate search questions in the office or laboratory of the clients they serve. For instance, Edith Dalton serves a consortium of special, academic, and public libraries called the Worcester (MA) Area Cooperating Libraries by taking her 13 pound TI 735 terminal to whichever institution the search patron is associated with. To a large extent, decisions of this kind will dictate the most logical physical location for support and clerical staff as well as for the computer terminals, search aids, and other facilities.

Another organizational matter to be decided is that of assigning specific responsibility for monitoring and managing the library's online services. Commonly, this assignment falls to a special coordinator, whose qualifications and duties are addressed more specifically below.

The final organizational element is that of deciding, in light of the anticipated level of demand for online services, how many professional-level personnel will be required, and what size clerical staff will be necessary to support them. Coupled with these decisions are those related to the specific qualifications, duties and responsibilities of each member of the online services group, and of course their professional and organizational relationships, including supervision, coordination, and possible lines of succession.

In some libraries, the anticipated work load emanating from such services will dictate that the people providing them will only be required to spend a certain percentage of their total work time in this connection.[1] In all libraries offering online services, however, some organizational provision should be made for competent and dependable back up staff, particularly for the active information service librarians.

One logical commonplace way of achieving this is to make sure that the online services coordinator keeps his or her searching skills up to date in a disciplined way. In larger organizations, one or more assistant coordinators should do the same.

PROVIDING PHYSICAL FACILITIES

The next undertaking to be addressed is that of arranging the physical facilities necessary to support the provision of online bibliographic search services. Some -- especially public -- libraries have chosen, at least initially, to place the library's computer terminal near the

---

[1] University of California at San Diego; Cornell University; and University of Toronto, Roberts Library to name a few.

main desk or in some other highly visible location, in hope of catching the interest of library patrons who are there on other business. The San Mateo County and the San Jose public libraries are among those who chose this course. It is now generally conceded, though, that it is better to locate the terminal and associated computer search facilities in a reasonably private spot -- ideally, in a separate room, as is done, for example, at the Dallas and Philadelphia public libraries. Often, the online services are located within the reference department of the library -- where they can be more easily integrated with other reference facilities. Moreover, the entire reference staff can be more actively involved in providing and supporting the online services -- and vice versa. James Bement of Xerox's Technical Information Center in Rochester says its terminal, at the reference desk, gets heavy use for "quick and dirty stuff" such as checking citations that can be done faster and more conveniently that way than by turning to the printed services.

Communications and Space

Fortunately, no elaborate site preparation is necessary. Even when the library elects to use relatively sophisticated video terminals, the installation typically consists of no more than unpacking the terminal, plugging it into a grounded electrical convenience outlet, and connecting it, via a black box called a modem (for modulator-demodulator), to a telephone line. It is best if this line is dedicated exclusively to provision of online services.

Aside from the terminal itself, the telephone link to the computer (and, where desired, a compact output printer), all that is really required is a modicum of furniture and amenities that will create a productive work environment. Obviously, the site must also provide the information services librarian with ready access to the necessary manuals, thesauri, and other search aids.

While any specific library may have to accommodate certain compromises, the services location chosen should be convenient to the reference staff and the reference collections, and reasonably accessible to patrons who might be interested in investigating what the service has to offer them. It should be out of the way enough to avoid interference from established traffic patterns or other activities of the library. Redwood City Public Library located its terminal in the main reference/reading room, but noise complaints from patrons soon forced installation of an acoustical cover. Naturally, the location chosen should be conducive to the interviews and other activities associated with preparing and evaluating searches.

The room or space dedicated to the online services should be adequate to allow a rearch specialist and one or two users to work freely at and around the terminal in some semblance of comfort, free of outside interruptions, and with a modicum of confidentiality. If possible, perhaps by rearranging a few pieces of furniture, there should be enough room around the terminal to accommodate small groups for demonstration purposes. There should also be room for files or shelves to accommodate related records, bibliographic search aids, and printed reference materials.

Work tables are generally better than desks, both because they afford the librarian and the user more leg room, and because the ample work surface is less likely to get cluttered up with the paper and other impedimenta that tend to accumulate on the desk tops. Sara D. Knapp of the State University of New York at Albany also notes that "while promoting joint collaboration, the table preserves a comfortable distance for those who find too much physical closeness distracting."[1] If a portable terminal is contemplated, a cart to facilitate its movement would be in order, and some librarians seem to be partial to a small rack to display the promotional brochures and other literature associated with the online services.

A few chairs that aren't too comfortable, lamps as necessary, ashtrays and other accessories, if appropriate, and the necessary manuals, retrieval aids, materials and supplies complete the picture. The matter of decorative touches we leave to the discrimination of the individual librarians and the tender mercies of the available budget.

Necessary utilities include a grounded (three pronged) 220 volt electrical outlet for each terminal, and a separate telephone line and number for each terminal's communications. In addition, it is advisable but not necessary to install a separate telephone line and number dedicated to communications between the library and its online user clientele and suppliers. This way, the institution and maintenance of online services will not be dependent on

---

[1] Knapp, Sara D., "The Reference Interview in the Computer Based Setting," RQ Summer, 1978.

availability of regular telephone circuits. Lighting, heating, air conditioning and ventilation levels at the online services location should be adequate, but need not be any different from those provided elsewhere in the active areas of the library.

Another consideration not to be overlooked is the security of the online services area. Thefts do occur; in fact the MEDLINE terminal at the University of Kentucky's medical library has been stolen twice. Elements to consider include at least the security of the terminal itself from theft, tampering, and unauthorized use, the security of the telephone communication lines, control of the integrity or privacy of manuals, supplies and other printed materials, including records and service files, and protection of the location, itself, from the hazards of fire, vandalism, and the like.

Signs pointing the way to the online site, and listings in various directories and handbooks, will help potential users to find the service.

The Computer Terminal

In terms of physical facilities, the most critical item is the computer terminal. While an exhaustive treatment of terminal features is beyond the purview of this report, a serious comparative study of what is available is certainly in order. The possibilities range from relatively pokey teletype terminals -- which many libraries consider unacceptably noisy -- to sleek, silent video terminals, some of them incorporating a full-fledged programmable mini or microcomputer. Optional features are available with most equipment to help adapt it to the special needs of each particular library.

Library managers totally new to the mysteries of terminal selection, and ignorant of the wide scope of choice available, generally seek outside advice. This can come from the institution's computer or data processing staff, from the supplier of the online retrieval services they have selected, from representatives of the manufacturers of the terminals themselves, or from experienced people in libraries that have already been providing online services for some time.[1] While these sources can provide insights,

---

[1] A useful discussion of terminal selection considerations, by expert Mark S. Radwin, appeared in the January and April, 1977 issues of ONLINE Magazine ("Choosing A Terminal," Parts I & II).

it is important not to impute to them more expertise, or broader familiarity with what's on the market, then they can really bring to the question. Moreover, once a particular terminal is decided upon, library managers are likely to want further expert advice on such matters as the intricacies and implications of leasing arrangements and maintenance contracts.

At minimum, those responsible for selecting a terminal will want to consider such factors as:

. Speed of operation, (and printing speed, if printout facilities are required);

. Operating noise levels;

. Ease of operation;

. The readability of the display screen presentation, in the case of video terminals;

. The number and variety of command keys;

. The actual portability, if a portable terminal is desired;

. Any ancillary equipment required to make the terminal compatible with the communication lines and the computer facilities of the data base processer;

. Reliability;

. The comprehensiveness, responsiveness, and cost of repair and service arrangements;

. The relative attractions of rental, leasing, and outright purchase;

. The terminal's ability to accommodate new data base suppliers that the library may want to consider; and of course

. Cost.

Other materials needed at the search site include:

. Handbooks, thesauri, and other manuals for the data bases and retrieval systems in question;

. Forms for logging in search requests, user profiles, search results, charges, and other administrative details;

. Printout paper, ribbons, miscellaneous supplies; and

. Promotional materials such as brochures, newsletters, or price lists that will explain the online services to potential patrons.

PERSONNEL SELECTION AND TRAINING

The sixth major start up consideration is the selection and training of the library personnel who will be providing the online services. Every member of the library staff should receive at least a general orientation to the new online services, the physical location in which they are provided, their relationship to the more conventional reference services provided by the library, and their contribution to the library's overall mission.

Ideally, every professional member of the reference department staff should be trained to interview patrons and to conduct online reference searches. In the best of all possible worlds, at least one of the information services librarians will hold a degree in each of the subject disciplines covered by the data bases being offered.

As a practical matter, of course, most libraries will have to make do with the human resources that are already aboard. Until the next generation of librarians finds its way into the profession, libraries will have to develop internally a cadre of information services librarians, starting with staff members who, in all probability, have never before switched on a computer terminal.

Fortunately, the task is not as formidable as it might seem. Except for the very rare library that can justify maintaining its own computer facilities to process data bases, the provision of online reference services is essentially a turnkey operation. The necessary equipment and facilities, programs, systems analysis and design, the generation or acquisition of data bases, the communications links, and all ancillary services are the concern of specialized outside vendors. These firms merely contract with the libraries to provide interactive online access to bibliographic data bases for a fee.

Accordingly, just as a driver is not required to understand internal combustion engines in order to operate the family car, an information services librarian does not have to master the intricacies of systems analysis, computer programming, and telecommunications, in order to operate the terminal and competently search remote data bases. Communicating by telephone is certainly a familiar activity, the keyboard of the computer terminal is very similar to that of a conventional typewriter. Further, the skills, insights and activities involved in providing computer-based reference services build upon the knowledge and skills that have long been in the repertoire of reference librarians.

Learning about data bases is very much along the lines of collection development. The structure, format, and other characteristics of the data bases echo those of the corresponding printed indexing and abstracting services. Moreover, compiling a unique bibliography for an individual does not differ fundamentally from compiling one for a group with identical interests. Thus, viewed merely as a tool for enhancing, augmenting, and extending the traditional activities of reference librarians, the computer terminal loses much of its mystique.

That said, however, relatively intensive initial training is nevertheless required, as is an ongoing effort on the part of information services librarians to stay abreast of new developments, and to maintain their proficiency in searching. Deft use of the terminal itself is a relatively minor factor in the overall efficiency and effectiveness of an online search. As Ann Ross, manager of the Business Library at G.D. Searle put it in an interview, "The difficulty with training is not memorizing buttons but showing people how online services fit in with their other tools."

Much more important than terminal proficiency are the librarian's interviewing and negotiating skills and the ability to devise an intelligent search strategy in response to a particular challenge. This being the case, candidates for training as information services librarians should be selected on the basis of their personality and intellectual power as well as their reference or subject matter backgrounds. Among the many attributes that searchers should possess, only a few seem to be more pertinent to online searching than to conventional research librarianship. Particularly important is the ability to relate to and communicate well with other specialists. Searchers should also have a strong service orientation, for they should see themselves as advocates of clientele needing information, not as keepers of the keys to the terminal.

Interest in the field is critical. Some librarians have found these new services vaguely threatening, and in the words of Kris Brooks of Oregon State University, "have de-selected themselves as search consultants." Others are uneasy in what is called the "machine interface," particularly where a typing or spelling error might be evident to a library patron that they are serving. Some dislike the pressure and unforgiving nature of the terminal, or simply resent using it. "I didn't go to library school to sit and type all day" one snapped. Other librarians lack the energy or inclination to undertake intensive retraining. Finally, some simply prefer the easy familiarity of traditional bibliographic tools to the structured ritual and intellectual demands of providing individualized reference service.

Types of Training

To say that training is required to convert a reference librarian into an accomplished information services librarian is not to say that the training has to be formal. In fact, results of the survey by Wanger et al indicate that, being avid readers almost by reflex, about half the librarians then functioning as online searchers simply collected various instruction manuals and whatever other literature came to hand, and curled up to teach themselves how to become information services librarians.

Among those lacking formal training, most librarians seem to have simply read the available literature and then practiced with the computer terminal until they felt confident enough to tackle their first search for a patron; others have been tutored by colleages who had been formally trained or had gained experience elsewhere. A number have taken advantage of the MEDLEARN program made available by the National Library of Medicine. Still other online searchers have had formal training during their professional education in a library school, as many courses now have incorporated hands-on training and expereince with online services (e.g. those at Syracuse University, University of California at Berkeley, Drexel University, UCLA, etc.)

The most popular source of formal training with online retrieval systems is, not surprisingly, the vendors of online retrieval systems.

The basic training courses offered by the online retrieval service vendors concentrate on manipulating the system itself; that is, logging on and off, submitting search and output commands, responding to system messages, and the like. Normally, there is only limited discussion of the peculiarities of particular data bases and of the best ways of exploiting them in the course of a search.

This omission works to the disadvantage of librarians in public and academic libraries. Unlike their counterparts in special libraries (especially corporate libraries), these librarians have less experience in doing reference searching for individual patrons, and less exposure to the indexing and abstracting tools of a particular discipline.

Nevertheless, the cost of the training from Lockheed, SDC, and now, BRS, is relatively low, the quality of instruction is high, and both competitive forces and the rapid growth in the number of academic libraries accessing these systems is likely to result in at least selected sections being expanded and more fully oriented to the needs of academic and public libraries.

In addition, the newsletters published by the principal online retrieval service vendors include valuable tips and techniques which make useful training aids. Also, the companies make available various instruction manuals and guidebooks.

Finally, a growing number of library schools offer short extension courses in online searching (in addition to the longer courses, at the schools mentioned earlier). Among those with workshops open to outsiders are the Universities of Arizona, Denver, Illinois, and Toronto, as well as Simmons College (Boston) and Rosary College (River Forest, IL).

While one can master the data bases and operating principles by diligent study, one can only become a proficient online searcher by being online. Learning to search data bases effectively can only be done through individual practice, online, at the computer terminal. A typical, well prepared reference librarian will probably require at least several hours of live connect time, practicing and interacting with the computer, exploring new possibilities, and refining skills and techniques, before the first search for a patron can be realistically attempted.

While a new searcher's learning curve rises very steeply at first, and then tends to flatten out, it can be expected to continue to rise throughout the first year. A number of studies confirm that experienced searchers are able to complete an online search considerably faster than a neophyte. Randolph Hock noted, for example, that between a new searcher's first and second month on the job at the University of Pennsylvania in Philadelphia, the average search time dropped by 11 minutes.[1]

Where feasible, new searchers can also learn a great deal by observing more experienced searchers working at the terminal. Opinion is divided on the question whether or not it is better for a new information services librarian to fully master one data base before trying to learn about others, but there is clearly merit in learning to use only one online retrieval system at a time. Subsequent ones can then be mastered much more quickly.

The value of advanced training, or refresher sessions, is also well established. "You can't learn it just once," cautions Xerox's Jim Bement. "I've been to three Predicast meetings on how to use their data base, and I go to SDC and Lockheed updates at least once a year. I always learn something new and useful. Searcher training is ongoing, and it must be. You learn when you need to know something. Manuals and first-time courses overload the newcomer. You need annual updates; you learn because your needs grow with experience." He's certainly not alone in that observation. Turning again to the Wanger survey: 96% of the searchers who had had some advanced training reported that they considered it to be useful, while 81% of those who had not had the benefit of such training were convinced that it would be useful.[2]

The major vendors of online retrieval services offer well thought out advanced courses of this kind, but a number of libraries are precluded from taking advantage of them, both because of the steep tuition fees and the associated transportation and accommodation expenses involved, and because of the internal disruption that would result from the absence of the search specialist attending the sessions. The gist of the information imparted in these advanced workshops will probably find its way into print, and therefore be more conveniently available to all who could benefit from it.

---

[1] Hock, R.E., "Providing Access to Externally Available Bibliographic Data Bases in an Academic Library," College & Research Libraries, 30 (May 1975)

[2] Wanger et al., op. cit.

Meanwhile, most information service librarians will have to keep themselves up to date by diligently reading vendors' newsletters and announcements, literature distributed by any groups or consortia with which their library may be affiliated, publications of the various professional societies serving the field, and such relevant publications as <u>Online Magazine</u>, <u>On-Line Review</u>, and <u>Messages from MARS</u>. Within budget limitations, attendance at seminars, workshops, symposia and conferences can also help information services librarians refine and hone their skills.

Interviewing Technique

One aspect of training that may get overlooked in the preoccupation with terminals and data bases is the need to prepare information services librarians for the pre-search interviews with patrons. Here, as with reference librarians who refer patrons to printed sources, the problem is to transform the patron's information need into a question that can be answered by one or more specific sources. The key difference is that with computer-based searches, the user delegates the actual search to the librarian.

Hence, the pre-search interview must describe the nature of the search services and the data bases available, elicit information about the patron's needs, and cast those needs into search statements using the vocabulary of the relevant data bases.

This process calls for sophisticated interviewing skills on the part of the information services librarian. It is not enough for the librarian to have familiarity with the service itself, and with the data bases offered; he or she also needs a manner that encourages efficient communication between patron and specialist. Thus, training should deal with techniques for conducting the interview, and with the effects of such non-verbal behavior as eye contact, tone of voice, and the like.

The technique of using video tapes or audio tapes to record and later analyze the interview process is being used more and more. Workshops at the Universities of Toronto, Denver, Pittsburgh, Washington, as well as at Syracuse and Drexel Universities, have concentrated on this aspect of online services. Tables 4-3 and 4-4 on the following pages reproduce forms used by the author for observation and analysis. Not all events occur during the interview, but some are regarded as essential to the success of the search.

TABLE 4-3: CHECKLIST FOR OBSERVING EVENTS

IN PRE-SEARCH INTERVIEW (ATHERTON)

DESCRIPTIVE

UD User Description
- a - Experience with computer searches
- b - Manual search techniques and experiences

SD System Description
- a - Search service
- b - Search procedures

DBS Data Base Selection
- a - Discussion of choices
- b - Choice made by Information Specialist

TA Tutorial Activity

Requested by User	Offered by Information Specialist
_____ System	_____ System
_____ Data Base	_____ Data Base
_____ Search Strategy	_____ Search Strategy

NEGOTIATION & CONSTRUCTION

CR Clarification of Request
- a - Offered by User
- b - Requested by Information Specialist
- c - Agreement on narrative statement of request (maybe prepared before interview and revised)

RN Request Negotiation
- a - User _discusses_ subject area terminology and _literature_ relevant to his/her research.
- b - Information Specialist _discusses_ retrieval system terminology, vocabulary, indexing practices
- c - Requirements to be imposed on output (date, language, etc.)
- d - Broader or narrower search?

VC Vocabulary Construction for Search
- a - Discuss free text search vs. controlled
- b - Terms _offered_ or rejected by user (prompted or volunteered)
- c - Terms _selected_ or rejected by Information Specialist (with or without user agreement?)
- d - Vocabulary aids consulted
- e - BT, NT, RT, synonyms, etc. reviewed
- f - Accepted or rejected terms (by either user or information specialist)
- g - Terms to be excluded.

TABLE 4-3: CHECKLIST FOR OBSERVING EVENTS
IN PRE-SEARCH INTERVIEW (ATHERTON)
CONTINUED

SS Search Strategy Formulation
- a - Logic formation <u>discussed</u> (and, or, not) broader or narrower.
- b - Concepts arranged in categories
- c - Strategies <u>formed</u> (with or without user agreement)
- d - Fields for searching decided
- e - Output formats and limits (No. of references) decided.

OTHER ACTIVITIES

DA Diverting Activity
- interruptions, conversation

OA Other Activities
- administrative (name, address, billing arrangements)
- explanation of costs
- arrangements for on-line session
- arrangements for post-search interview
- user's use of output

TABLE 4-4: CHECKLIST FOR OBSERVING INTERPERSONAL COMMUNICATION DURING PRE-SEARCH INTERVIEW (ATHERTON)

INFORMATION SPECIALIST	USER
Positive Occurrences	
Initially, used open questions	Freely stated information need
*Encouraged discussion	
Answered questions in understandable way	Asked questions freely
Thoughtful pauses before answering	
Summarized or paraphrased request	Appeared confident in skill of information specialist
Listened to user	Listened to information specialist
*Gave full attention	*Gave full attention
Remained objective about subject of request	
Appeared comfortable and relaxed	Appeared comfortable and relaxed
Negative Occurrences	
Initially, used closed questions	Had to be prompted to give information
	Changed topic often
	Showed indecision about choices
*Interrupted or talked-over often	*Frequently interrupted or talked-over
Gave command or directives, expecting compliance	Objected to suggested strategies
Attempted to demonstrate superior knowledge	Exhibited insufficient knowledge about subject
*Placed user on defensive	*Placed information specialist on defensive
*Gave erratic attention	
Reacted subjectively to request	
Exhibited uneasiness	Exhibited uneasiness
Appeared competitive	Appeared competitive
Appeared submissive	Appeared submissive
Ended interview prematurely	Terminated interview prematurely
Seemed annoyed	Seemed annoyed

Training for Non-Searchers

Also important in the start up of online services is training for those not actually conducting searches. A brief orientation for professional librarians not actually engaged in searching can help them understand its role, and deal with patrons' requests for information. Training for clerical staff who will be engaged in related tasks, such as manning the information desk, scheduling appointments, or handling billing, may also be advisable.

CONCLUSION

This chapter has tried to give the flavor of the many administrative and professional considerations required to launch online reference services. Once the initial decision has been made, the library administrator is faced with the need to establish the mission of the service, analyze the potential user market, allocate needed resources, provide organization and physical facilities, and train the specialists who will carry on the service.

In a period of enormous pressure on library budgets, the financial aspects of online services quickly come to fore. Almost no institution can afford to completely subsidize searches for its patrons, and the various ways of charging are complex and controversial. Chapter 5 will deal with these issues.

5
Financial Considerations

In light of the special nature and the considerable expense of providing online bibliographic reference services, it is surprising that some organizations providing these services do not maintain separate budget and accounting systems. Even among those that do, budget and accounting procedures are rarely comprehensive. While this phenomenon may reflect a lack of appreciation for the function and value of such financial tools, or an out-and-out distaste for the discipline they require, it seems to be linked to a feeling that if the library is recovering at least the direct, identifiable, incremental costs of serving patrons with these new services, no special budgeting or accounting is required.

Such an argument is specious, under the best of circumstances, but it is particularly weak in light of the fact that in too many libraries, the direct costs that they have in mind are restricted to those for which the library is invoiced, in connection with each search, by the vendors of the communication and retrieval services. Typically, these include computer connect time, usage fees by communications suppliers, such as Tymshare, and the cost of offline printing of the citations and abstracts retrieved by the search.

Taken together, however, these costs constitute only the tip of a substantial iceberg, ignoring, as they do, even such allied incremental costs as telephone service from the terminal to the nearest node of the time-shared network, and the internal cost of online printing of a limited number of citations right at the terminal. More importantly, each individual search has associated with it a proportional share of the significant costs incurred by the library in the equipment, facilities, and talent necessary to make the search possible.

Whether or not a particular library intends to recover from users all, or even a fraction, of these very real imputed and associated costs, it seems clear that not even recognizing their existence, and making provision for them in a specific budgeting and accounting system, is simply unrealistic.

The scope and detail of the accounting provisions for online services that are appropriate in a given library depend, of course, on the circumstances. By and large, it is preferable to keep things as simple as possible, particularly with respect to those aspects of the matter that will be visible to the library's patrons.

At one end of the spectrum of possible choices, there have been a number of libraries, including Oregon State University, that were not required to develop any kind of budget at all for instituting online systems.[1] Money was simply transferred to the activity from other programs or categories of the overall budget as start-up expenses were incurred. It is unlikely, however, that many organizations can long afford to treat so expensive an innovation in so cavalier a fashion. Moreover, it seems probable that even the libraries that were able to inaugurate online services in this way have since been required to convert the insights of their first few months or year of operation into more disciplined statements of the amounts and allocation of funds that they will need in subsequent years.

At the other end of the spectrum are libraries that have chosen, or have been required, to develop extremely detailed budgets and accounting entries, e.g. UCLA and University of Rochester. While there may be merit in such arrangements at larger institutions, chances are that until the library has hard experience, entries for a number of the line items will initially have to consist of estimates and perhaps outright guesses.

The most common approach to developing a budget, at least for the first year of operation, seems to be that of forcasting the cost of an average online search, based on the so called "out of pocket" costs (communications, computer time, and off line printing). This is then multiplied by the number of searches anticipated during the course of the first year. The result is regarded as a tentative budget for online services.

A number of studies have been made and reported in the literature that purport to have isolated the cost of an average online search at a particular library, or a group

---

[1] University of California at San Diego and State University of New York at Oswego are other examples.

of libraries. For example, more than 60% of the library managers who cooperated with the SDC survey by Wanger et al., estimated that the average cost per search in their libraries was under $30.00. Similarly, other researchers have reported[1] that at the four public libraries in the San Francisco area taking part in the DIALIB experiment, a study of 411 "free" (to the patron) online bibliographic searches in the spring of 1975, cost an average of $28.41 each, exclusive of telephone line charges.

Unfortunately, such numbers are virtually meaningless from a pragmatic point of view, and they certainly cannot be generalized beyond the specific institutions involved. The difficulties in drawing inferences from such figures are legion, beginning with the fact that the statistical average may not be remotely typical, depending on the range of the underlying data. In the case of the SDC study, for example, the specific estimates of cost per search range from $1.00 (!) to $100.00, with nearly as many managers estimating the cost at $50.00 or more as placed it at between $20.00 and $30.00.

Moreover, in many such studies, including the two just cited, the cost averages represent an aggregate cutting across many data bases with individual access fees ranging from $25.00 to $150.00 per hour. This range of costs certainly skewed the DIALIB data, as patrons of these public libraries -- many of whom were college students -- show a marked affinity for ERIC, one of the cheapest data bases.

The SDC results are probably similarly skewed by the fact that many of the cooperating libraries were accessing the very inexpensive, heavily subsidized, government data bases as well as those of commercial suppliers, and the cost differences can be dramatic. As one example: in addition to very low cost computer connect time, the MEDLINE service, operated by the National Library of Medicine, offers citations printed offline for 10 cents per _page_, as contrasted with the fees of 10 cents to 50 cents per _citation_ levied by the commercial services.

The skill and experience of the searchers also play a major roll. Obviously, a seasoned search librarian in a special library, who runs several searches per day against

---

[1] Cooper, Michael D., and DeWath, Nancy A., technical report, _The Cost of On-line Bibliographic Searching_, Applied Communication Research, Dec. 1975.

the same data base, will be able to complete a given search faster and at lower cost than a counterpart in an academic library who is asked to browse through that particular data base no more than once per month -- or per year.

The most important reason that these specious "average cost per search" figures become very elastic yardsticks, though, is the fact that major cost elements are almost routinely ignored. Typically, an online search is conceived of as beginning when the computer terminal is switched on, and ending when the terminal is switched off at the end of the search. This disregards the fact that a particular search may require two or more sessions at the terminal. (In fact, at Bell Labs, a search takes an _average_ of two sessions, and often takes three.)

Some observers limit the definition of an online search even more narrowly, contending that a search consists of a single formulation run against a single data base. Still others more realistically recognize that the time spent at a terminal represents only a portion of the time required to develop and conduct a successful search. An interview between the information services librarian and the user, to define goals and strategy, must precede the search. Also, in most cases, additional staff effort must follow the search; e.g., a review and assessment of the results by the librarian, possibly another interview with the user to go over the results, and perhaps an extension of the search to print media or to data bases available online from another vendor. The librarian may also have to edit, reorganize, and package the results before sending them on to the user.

Even when the scope of what constitutes a single search has been settled, there is still wide disagreement between different libraries as to what items ought to be included in the computation of average search costs. There is consensus that the costs of offline printing, communications, and of computer-related fees, or connect time, should be taken into account. But opinions diverge over such issues as prorating the costs of acquiring or renting the computer terminal; the organization's overhead costs, such as utilities and space; the costs of basic data base service subscriptions, or minimal fees, paid to suppliers; and of the professional and clerical staff time involved in providing searches.

Relatively few libraries include in their calculations library staff time, even when the searcher's time can be

accurately linked to a particular search. Overhead costs --
again even such elements as can be attributed to a particular
search such as paper for the online printer, postage, and
photocopies of the output citations -- are also rarely included
in cost-per-search estimates.

For a host of reasons, then, we consider the popular
approach of developing a budget on the basis of "average
cost per search" multiplied by a speculative forecast of how
many searches might be anticipated, to be questionable at
best. It might result in some embarrassment if it were in
fact questioned by someone challenging the budget figures.
If, in the absence of any direct experience, the number initially used as the average cost per search is simply borrowed
from the published results of a cost survey made at another
institution, a budget arrived at in this way could be both
deceptive and invalid.

BUDGETING

We submit that a more appropriate approach is to estimate
each relevant expenditure anticipated, both initially and during the ensuing six to 12 months, and then to derive the cost
per search by applying each of these expenses to the projected
search load. During the course of the projection, it would
be prudent to allow for escalation in the costs of some supplies
and services, as well as discounts for increased usage.

Start-up expenditures would include at least the cost of
acquiring a computer terminal either by lease, rental, or
purchase (the latter probably running between $2000 and $4000);
the installation charge for the terminal telephone line and
the electrical outlet, if one is required; ancillary equipment,
such as a modem or acoustic coupler; and computer, telephone,
and other charges associated with inaugural demonstrations
to prospective users. In addition there is the cost of such
partitions, furniture, fixtures, and decoration as may be
required for the service site area; manuals, thesauri, and
other retrieval aids; perhaps a microform reader; and an
initial supply of forms, stationery, promotional materials,
etc. Finally, there will be training costs for the cadre of
searchers, including travel and lodging costs where required;
the cost of equipment repair and service contracts; and any
front-end connect or service charges levied by the vendors that
will be used.

The recurring, or ongoing, costs are generally categorized
as either direct or indirect. Direct costs are taken to be

those for which the library is invoiced by the retrieval system vendors, and which therefore are directly attributable to specific searches, assuming that the library has its logs in order. Initially, of course, these will have to be estimated, based at least in part on the known experiences of the most comparable library that accesses the bases for a similar clientele. These costs include computer connect time, communications time, offline printing, and, in some states, sales taxes.

It is important to recognize, however, that some charges appearing on vendor invoices may be difficult or impossible to associate with a particular search. Whether or not the library intends to recover such costs, they are undeniably incurred, and should be accounted for and budgeted. Among the charges that would fall into this category are those for regularly demonstrating the system to potential users and for internal use of the computer by the library staff, either for reference or training purposes. Other such charges include those for replacement printouts when the originals get lost in the mail, and for aborted searches resulting from a mistake on the part of the information service librarian. There are also likely to be charges for such online "housekeeping" chores as getting search help or system status reports from the vendor and for storing certain search modules in the computer for later use on other searches.

The indirect costs of online search services are those not evidenced by invoices from retrieval service vendors. Some such costs are fixed, and remain largely the same irrespective of the volume of the searching being done; and others are variable, their level rising or falling with the number of searches being performed.

The principal indirect costs include the rental or depreciation and maintenance charges for the terminal; telephone charges; and consumable supplies such as postage, stationery and printout paper, forms and promotional material. Other indirect costs are incurred for new and updated search aids during the course of the year, for internal photocopying of such material as journal articles of interest to searchers and administrative memos and the like, and for training of the professional staff. General overhead, such as space, utilities, custodial service, depreciation, and both clerical and professional staff time also constitute indirect costs.

One rule of thumb used in calculating the staff time is that an information services librarian must devote approximately one hour to each search, including the time spent in pre-search interviews, in formulating and running the search, in filling out the log book, and in processing the citation printout. In addition, for each search performed, the librarian is likely to have to spend another 15 minutes on activities related to the online search services, such as studying manuals and newsletters, conferring with colleagues, attending meetings, giving demonstrations, and enhancing or extending search skills.[1]

Clerical support typically takes the form of typing, checking invoices, calculating statistics, mailing printouts or notifying patrons that printouts are ready for pick up at the library, requisitioning supplies, etc.

When each of these costs is isolated (or estimated) and toted up the library will have a reasonable budget for its online services. When they are prorated over a realistic estimate of search volume, the library will have some notion of what "average cost per search" can be anticipated.

With the expenditures of online services estimated, the library can turn its attention to sources of funding. While grants and special appropriations have been fairly commonly used to fund the inauguration of online search services, these sources have a distressing way of diminishing, or drying up entirely, once the operation is in full swing. This is particularly so if initial results do not measure up to expectations, as was evidently the case at the Redwood City and Brooklyn public libraries.

New funds, everyone's first choice as the source of online support, are not always forthcoming, although each library's situation is in some ways unique. Funds reallocated from conventional reference services or other library activities can usually be had, but never, it seems, in the quantities required. Some universities -- Dartmouth, for example -- have been able to fund their online search services by allocating some or all of the costs to the major departments of the university whose faculty can demonstrably benefit from the service. Major corporations, too, can distribute the cost of online search services between several benefiting departments, sometimes via a formal system of internal charges. Corporate practices vary widely. Bell Labs charges internal users only for searches that cost

---

[1] M.D. Cooper and Nancy DeWath, "The Cost of On-Line Bibliographic Searching." *Journal of Library Automation*, 9:3 (Sept. 1976).

more than $25.00, whereas the Warner Lambert/Parke Davis Pharmaceutical Research Division does not charge at all for specific searches. In contrast to both, the Xerox Technical Information Center tries to recover the full cost of a search, including overhead, by charging it back to the requester's unit.

USER FEES

Some special, and most academic and public, libraries however, find that in order to sustain the service at the present time, they must levy direct user charges to recover at least their direct costs of providing the service, and in some cases, a significant portion of the indirect costs as well. Even in the case of libraries such as State University of New York in Albany, that feel comfortable absorbing all costs of providing online search services, there may well be merit in instituting at least a "nuisance charge" to restrict usage of the system to a serious clientele. This also helps prevent overburdening not only the search staff but the photocopy, interlibrary loan, and circulation departments of the library as well. Unfortunately, there are certain students, scholars, and researchers who will cheerfully abuse any service that they perceive as being free. (On the other hand, Sara Knapp, of the Albany Library of the State University of New York notes that "The idea of imposing user fees to prevent abuse has itself been abused.")

It's certainly true that user fees for library services are not without their drawbacks. The most widely recognized of these is that such fees fly in the face of decades of tradition. Another difficulty is that user fees, particularly those aimed at recovering a substantial fraction of the true costs, tend to put online services out of reach of many potential users.[1] People without a grant, contract, departmental or company budget with which to pay the fees must forego the service.

---

[1] A careful and inclusive study of actual costs recorded at the Exxon Research and Engineering Co. library in Floral Park, NJ concluded that the true full cost of an average online search there is $112.00. Collette, A.D. and J.A. Price "A Cost/Benefit Evaluation of Online Interactive Bibliographic Searching in a Research and Engineering Organization" in The Value of Information, collected papers of the 1977 midyear meeting of ASIS, Syracuse University, pp. 24-30.

Another disadvantage is the added time lag imposed by the need to submit and process purchase requests. There is also no doubt that user fees impose on the library additional accounting, billing, collection, and possibly refund activities, and that user fees do restrict the number of patrons taking advantage of this service, particularly if it had earlier been available free.

It can even be argued that user fees, particularly substantial ones, can have an adverse impact on the quality of the searching being done. In the interest of saving money, a patron may accept a less comprehensive search, or fewer citations, than would otherwise be desirable.. Equally important, information service librarians are acutely aware of the pressure of mounting user charges, and may therefore be disinclined to probe a problem in greater depth or to pursue a search along additional channels. Inexperienced searchers are likely to be particularly uncomfortable about this, feeling that their lack of finesse may be forcing the patron to pay a premium for inefficient work.

Be that as it may, this is not the best of all possible worlds, and in many -- probably most -- libraries, the alternative to imposing user fees is to forego providing online services altogether. Besides, user fees have two important incidental benefits for the library: they demonstrate the demand for and reception of the online services, and they facilitate cost accounting and control.

User fees can be determined and structured in a number of ways, depending on the circumstances. The simplest, and perhaps the most common, approach is essentially to pass on to the patron, in the form of a user fee, the direct costs incurred by the library in serving him or her, that is, computer, communications, and printing costs. An increasing number of libraries are going beyond this, however, to recover at least some of the additional costs associated with providing the online service.

Elements included in these additional fees range from a pro rata share of the terminal cost and other investments made to start up and maintain the service, to a share of such ongoing expenses as telephone, supplies and postage, and a share of any incremental overhead costs. Such costs may show up in the form of a separate service fee charged for each search. One example of this is the $5.00 per hour surcharge levied by Oregon State University on searches done for academics from other schools. Non-academic outsiders pay $15.00 per hour surcharge. Another example is shown on the following page.

An alternative approach is to add a small increment to the charge per minute of computer connect time, or to incorporate the fee into the library's basic charge for making the search. The Dallas Public Library has imbedded about $1.00 per minute, over and above the direct costs it incurs, into its per-minute structure of fees. These fees, which vary according to the specific data base being queried, come into play only when a search takes longer than 10 minutes of computer connect time. Searches that take 10 minutes or less each cost the patron $25.00, regardless of the data base used.

Some libraries may want to go a step further, adding a specific charge for the time spent by the information services librarian in actually conducting the search at the terminal. The ultimate would be to also charge for the staff time spent in interviewing the patron and formulating the search, and in subsequently analyzing and editing the results. While hardly a popular approach, this more or less full-cost recovery approach is used in some major corporate research libraries, where the "charge" is passed to the budget of the department requesting the service. Full cost recovery tends to minimize the cuts in other services that otherwise have to be made in order to add online services. Since the online services are then fundamentally self-sustaining, they can grow at whatever rate is warranted by patron demand.

An increasing number of libraries divide their fee structure, offering patrons a choice of either standard searches, or what are variously called "special" or "custom" searches or something of that sort. A standard search is a relatively simple search, sometimes against only a single data base but more often constrained only with regard to connect time and the number output citations. For example, Stanford University divides the data bases it makes available into five categories, roughly according to the connect time fees charged by the retrieval service vendors. For a standard search, a patron may select any one of the data bases within a price group, and for the basic fee associated with that price, can get a standard search run against that data base, with up to 25 citations in the resulting bibliography.

The basic fees range from $13.00 to $36.00, depending on the price category of the data base selected. The basic

TABLE 5-1: FEE SCHEDULE, UNIVERSITY OF CALIFORNIA, SAN DIEGO

The University Libraries
University of California, San Diego
La Jolla, California 92093
Charges for On-Line Computerized Literature Searches
Processed by the UCSD Library

The cost of an on-line search is the sum of the DATA BASE ACCESS COSTS and the SERVICE FEE. DATA BASE ACCESS COSTS vary depending on the data base being searched, as outlined below. The SERVICE FEE is determined by the user's status (i.e., UCSD, Educational, or Other as defined below).

DATA BASE ACCESS COSTS:

There is a flat fee charged for searches of the following data bases.*

    AGRICOLA (formerly NAL/CAIN) (Agriculture)................$7.00
    BIOSIS PREVIEWS (Biology).................................$7.00
    CHEMICAL ABSTRACTS CONDENSATES (Chemistry)................$7.00
    ERIC (Education)..$7.00
    INFORM (Business)...$7.00
    INSPEC (Physics; Computers; Electronics)..................$9.00
    NTIS (Government Reports).................................$7.00
    PYSCHOLOGICAL ABSTRACTS (Psychology) $9.00

For all other data bases (e.g., GEOREF, ENERGYLINE, FOUNDATION GRANTS INDEX, etc.), the requester pays for actual computer time and off-line print charges as billed to the UCSD Library by data base service companies.

SERVICE FEE:

User Status	Amount of Fee
UCSD Users (Students, faculty, and staff)	$3.00 per search**
Educational Users (Faculty and full-time students at colleges and universities other than UCSD; students enrolled at other UC campuses; UC Alumni Association members; Individual members of Friends of UCSD Library; University Extension students and faculty; members of the Chancellor's Club)	$10.00 per search**
Commercial, Government, Private, and Other Users (All individuals not covered by the above categories)	$25.00 per search (20 percent discount on service fee for this category when billed through SD-METRO*** member organization)

*The flat fee includes fifty references printed off-line. References in addition to the first fifty are charged for at the rate of $.05 each.
**For purposes of determining the service fee, a search consists of the searching of one topic on one data base. The searching of one topic on two data bases is also one search. The searching of two topics on one data base is two searches.
***San Diego Greater Metropolitan Area Library and Information Council

EXAMPLE

A UCSD student requests a BIOSIS PREVIEWS search and wants a maximum of fifty references DATA BASE ACCESS COST is $7.00. SERVICE FEE is $3.00. Total cost to student is $10.00.

fee is payable regardless of the number of citations from zero to 25. If more than 25 citations are available and desired, the customer is charged for these at an additional fee of between 10 cents and 50 cents per citation.

By contrast, custom searches are not provided at a fixed price. Instead, the patron is charged by the minute for the connect time, and is charged also for each citation, although an unlimited number of them may be acquired. In addition to these costs, each custom search carries an administrative fee of $2.00. Finally, while the cost of library time and overhead is absorbed for Stanford customers, these costs too are passed on to outsiders who request a custom search.

Similarily, at the University of Pennsylvania library in Philadelphia, patrons are offered the option of a standard search, at a fixed price, or what is called a special search. Standard searches are provided at a flat rate, with up to 50 citations being included in this base price. Patrons are permitted to select up to 10 descriptors (somewhat more, in the case of certain data bases) and the search is confined to a single data base. Patrons who insist on using more input terms or receiving additional citations are accommodated at an additional cost of 25 cents per term and 10 cents per citation, respectively. The library patron is not present when a standard search is being run.

Special searches, in which the patron actively participates, are not restricted with regard to cost, the number of input terms, or the number of output citations. These are typical, interactive searches -- again, normally against a single data base -- and the user pays a set fee per minute, as well as a small charge per citation retrieved.

The education library of another university offers three categories of standard search. Accessing only ERIC and Psychological Abstracts data bases, the library charges $5.00 for a simple online search. The fee covers the negotiation and refinement of search terms, and an online search of either file of up to 10 minutes, along with an online printout of up to 10 citations (excluding abstracts).

The second category of service is called a full search. For $10.00 this buys the same service as an online search plus the offline printout of up to 50 citations, with full abstracts, mailed to the user.

The third category is a special search package, at $15.00. This consists of search negotiation and an online search of both files, plus the offline printout of up to 50 citations with full abstracts from each file.

Patrons whose needs cannot be met with these standard searches can extend the search time of any of them for a fee of 50 cents for each additional minute beyond the original 10, and an incremental charge of five cents per citation beyond 50 -- again, printed offline.

This fee structure applies to all campus patrons of the library and to certain other users from non-profit institutions. Customers associated with profit-making organizations are charged an additional $10.00 "service fee."

The University of Kentucky is one of few institutions that applies a single fee structure to all comers. It is common practice, both among academic libraries and among the few special libraries that will accommodate outsiders, to impose higher fees on them. Such surcharges -- 50% in the case of Dartmouth, for instance, and a flat $25.00 at the University of California at San Diego -- are usually designed to recapture the full cost of providing an online search, specifically including staff time and overhead. In some cases, the fees are set to yield a modest profit, which is characteristically used to subsidize online searches for students.

The University of California at Berkeley adds $20.00 per search to its fee schedule when serving patrons who are not associated with the university. The fee structure for this library's standard searches is predicated on an average connect time of about 20 minutes. Experience indicates that standard searches generally require between 10 and 20 minutes, but they may take up to 30 minutes of connect time. Once under way, standard searches are permitted to exceed this bogey, but in that case, the patron may be charged overtime for each additional minute.

The cost of a standard search ranges from $15.00 to $60.00 an hour depending on the data bases selected and disregarding the artificially cheap MEDLINE family of data bases. Output citations, printed offline, are charged for separately, except in the case of searches against the New York Times Information Bank, where the first 50 citations are included in the standard search fee. The library considers 40 or more planned search terms the "break point" between a standard search and a special one. The standard search fee consists of the cost of computer connection to the particular data base, plus communications, plus $5.00 per search to cover certain indirect costs. This library absorbs such costs as overhead and the professional and clerical staff time.

Clearly, user fees for online bibliographic services can range from zero to $100.00 or more. The underlying cost recovery objectives can range from specious to comprehensive. The resulting fee structures run the gamut from simple to complex, and both the searches themselves and the patrons who utilize them can be categorized in a number of different ways. Each library must decide what arrangements make sense in light of its particular mission, economic circumstances and the clientele it serves.

A library that imposes hefty fees for these services runs the risk of discouraging potential users, while the interest and the skills of its searchers atrophy for lack of exercise, and internal pressures increase to shift financial support to other library activities. On the other hand, a library that imposes token fees, or none at all, runs the risk of being inundated by an increasing user clamor, not only for more online searching, but for a blizzard of full-text photo and fiche copies, heavy interlibrary borrowing, and an urgent re-examination of established collections.[1] Meanwhile, resistance builds to funding a larger staff to support so catastrophically expensive an operation. Each library must decide where to position itself at or between these two extremes.

OTHER FINANCIAL CONSIDERATIONS

With a detailed budget in place, based on realistic cost estimates, and with the thorny issue of user charges resolved in some pragmatic way, the library administration can turn its attention to the remaining financial considerations. These include at least:

. Establishing accounts payable procedures, including provision for detailed review of invoices, authorization for payment, and a classification for expenditures;

. Establishing procedures for handling delinquent accounts, refunds, and other contingencies;

. Determining when low cost or free introductory services will be terminated;

---

[1] Safeguards against such abuse can be found. Examples exist in the way in which computing center accounts are monitored in academic institutions.

• Scheduling a time to re-examine pricing policies, revenue and expenditures; and

• Establishing an acceptable protocol for instituting price changes.

Mechanisms for payment and collection procedures will have to be set up in every library. These might have to provide provision for accommodating some, or some combination of, the following: cash, checks, credit cards, subscription or other internal accounts, deposit accounts, formal purchase orders, and internal requisitions.

To minimize the financial complications between the library and its patrons, many libraries require, as a matter of policy, that users pay in full for standard searches at the time they request them. Users requesting a custom search are obliged to pay in advance a fee equal to that of a standard search, with the balance payable upon receipt of the off-line citations.

Other libraries try to protect themselves by merely requiring that library patrons sign a statement, when they request a search, acknowledging that they are committed to paying for the search even though it may yield few or no citations, or may in some other way be perceived of by the patron as unsatisfactory (see example on the following page). While such procedures and requirements may not be appropriate everywhere, they do establish at least an informal contractual arrangement and head off a certain number of misunderstandings.

Two final points should be touched upon before we leave the matter of financial considerations. The first is that some thought should be given to the potential "fallout" impact of online retrieval services on financial requirements elsewhere in the library. For example, it is important to recognize that the library must still maintain, and in some cases even enhance, its manual searching tools and capability. Some data bases contain no abstracts at all, and searchers will have to turn to printed products to obtain them.

Printed resources may also be needed to search the literature published in years prior to those included in the computer's data base. They are also important sources of detailed bibliographic data for interlibrary loan requests, for manually conducting simple searches that would not be economically justified online, for conducting certain kinds of searches that are more efficiently handled through the

TABLE 5-2: CHARGE FORM, UNIVERSITY OF CALIFORNIA, SAN DIEGO

The University Libraries   University of California, San Diego   La Jolla, California 92093

AUTHORIZATION TO CHARGE FOR COMPUTERIZED LITERATURE SEARCH

I hereby request a computerized literature search and agree to pay the UCSD Library for performing the search. I realize that the UCSD Library cannot guarantee that references of interest will be retrieved or that those which are retrieved will be highly relevant. I also understand that neither the service fee nor the prorated costs of a search are refundable once the search has been processed.

Signed: _____   Date: _____

PLEASE PRINT
Name: _____   Telephone: _____

Title or Position: _____   Department: _____

Mailing Address: _____

_____

I wish to pay in the following way:

_____ Please charge against the following UCSD budget number: _____

_____ I will pay by check or money order. (Note: The service fee is payable at the time the search is requested. A check or money order for the balance of the cost must be received by the Library Reference Department from which you requested the search before the results of the search will be released. Please make all checks payable to "Regents of the University of California.")

_____ Please bill me. (Note: Only institutions and corporate bodies--e.g., libraries, business firms, schools--and members of the San Diego Medical Society may be billed.)

Please Note:

The total charge for a computerized literature search run by the UCSD Library is the sum of two separate charges: a service fee and the prorated costs. The service fee varies according to the status of the user. The prorated costs are those for off-line prints and computer connect time (Note: Computer connect time is charged for by the minute; a fraction of a minute counts as a full minute for charging purposes). The prorated costs of searches vary greatly, depending on the topic and data base being searched, and cannot be calculated until after the search is processed. The average prorated costs of a search are about $15.00.

Please indicate if you have a maximum amount that you wish to spend: _____
The Library will make every effort to honor this maximum, but cannot guarantee to do so.

_____

LIBRARY USE ONLY

Request Taken By: _____   Unit: _____

Search Run By: _____   Date: _____

File(s) Searched: _____   Search Number(s) _____

CLSS 10   Total amount due: $_____   UCSD Libr.

structure and vocabulary of the printed materials, and of course, for providing back-up capability when the computer system is down or otherwise unavailable. (Notice though that print materials used only for back-up and supplementary details can be in the form of microfiche, enabling the library to save hundreds of linear feet of shelf space formerly needed for paper indexes.)

Another example of indirect financial impact is the increased demand for full-text documents that typically accompanies the introduction of online services. This may well require the library to increase its holding of journals, to cope with a significant increase in photocopying and inter-library loan activity, and perhaps to acquire additional microfiche facilities.

The final financial consideration is one of perspective. Expensive as it is to provide online services, neither the initial investment, nor the ongoing operating costs involved, play a hingepin role in most special and academic libraries. In the 18 institutions that were affiliated with the Northeast Academic Science Information Center, online data base services generally accounted for less than 1% of their total library expenditures.[1] (They do, of course, represent highly _visible_ expenditures.)

---

[1] Wax, David M; "NASIC and The Information Services Librarian: Room In the Middle" in _Proceedings of the 1975 Clinic on Library Applications of Data Processing_, ed. by F. Wilfred Lancaster, (Urbana: University of Illinois, 1976). p. 83.

6
Modes of Operation and Service Procedures

The scope and nature of the online bibliographic services that any given library will provide, will vary with the library. In each institution, policy and operating decisions must be made, with a view toward meeting perceived unmet information needs of patrons served by the library.

TYPES OF SERVICE TO BE OFFERED

Potential users of the online services will have to be specifically identified, and perhaps categorized, or ranked, in some order of service precedence or priority. In theory, the fundamental range of choices open to a library includes, at the one extreme, doing nothing whatever about online services, and at the other, processing machine-readable data bases on an in-house computer facility. As a practical matter, though, most libraries must choose from among three more moderate options.

The first is merely to refer users to online bibliographic search services at other locations.

The second basic option is to train staff to conduct pre-search interviews, while forwarding the actual search for processing at another institution. With relatively little effort, after his or her initial qualification, an able and enthusiastic reference librarian can perform this surrogate or intermediary role very well. This enables the library to make the benefits of online searching available to its clientele at minimum cost to the library, while building experience against the day when a more ambitious approach to providing online services can be justified.

The third fundamental option, and the one on which this work concentrates, is that of offering online search services directly, via communication links with one or more of the established vendors of data base retrieval services.

Assuming that this fundamental choice has been made, the library immediately faces a series of other decisions. Should the service be confined initially to one group of users, and/or to one or a few data bases, while the library gains experience? Alternatively, should the library at once offer access to many data bases, in the hope of attracting quickly as much patronage as is possible?

Even when the decision is taken to offer immediate access to a variety of data bases, there may be merit in confining these offerings to those available from a single retrieval system. This way, searchers can get comfortable with the commands, constraints, and quirks of one system before having to master subsequent ones.

The specific types of online search services to be offered must also be decided upon: retrospective, current awareness or both. If current awareness searches are to be offered, a further decision must be made with regard to whether the user profiles will be periodically re-entered, or will be stored in the computer and automatically re-run each time the relevant data bases are updated.

The provision of online access to statistical and other substantive data bases is outside the scope of this book, but might well fall within the scope of online services that a particular library may want to consider. Similarly, taking a broader view of computer-based bibliographic search services, a number of libraries, in deciding on the scope of services that they will provide, might give consideration to providing supplemental offline reference services, via one or more of the information processing centers that offer them.

The final variable to be settled, is the extent to which full-text documents will be provided, and how that will be done. Many libraries, reasoning that the user's real objective is information, rather than citations or abstracts, consider the provision of full-text documents an integral part of their reference services. Dallas Public Library and the Xerox Technical Information Center are in this camp. Others feel that once the search has been completed, and the patron has been provided with an edited list of pertinent citations, the patron is on his own to track down the necessary full-text documents. This is the view taken at Bell Laboratories Information Center, which conducts high-level online searches but refers users to the Bell Labs network of 24 technical libraries for full-text materials.

Still other libraries choose a middle ground. For example, the Stanford libraries accompany each bibliography with a short statement guiding the patron to the location of full-text documents; referring, for example, to the Union List of Serials for journals, periodicals, and magazines, proceedings of conferences and symposia and the like, to the card catalog for books, and to the interlibrary loan desk for materials not in the Stanford collection. An example of the type of cover sheet with which State University of New York in Albany presents citation printouts to users of its online services is shown on the following page.

As noted in Chapter 3, interlibrary loan traffic in full-text documents and photocopies inevitably intensifies as online retrieval systems are instituted and patrons begin seeking documents that correspond to new-found citations.

TIME AND LOCATION OF SERVICE

The next operational matter to be determined is the locations and times at which online retrieval services will be available. Most universities seem to join Kentucky, Dartmouth, and Oregon State in favoring a convenient central location, with the various administrative and economic advantages that offers. Others -- particularly the very large ones such as UCLA -- have opted to disperse the service. In this case, at least the negotiation of search terms and parameters, and the formulation of the search are handled by a subject specialist in each of the major departmental libraries (medicine, social sciences, agriculture etc.).[1]

Some institutions have gone further, establishing terminals and direct, online services in certain of these specialized satellite libraries. While such an approach has a certain number of advantages, it does require careful coordination and cooperation, including the intelligent cross-referral of users between these specialized units, and it complicates such administrative duties as accounting and cost control. After an initial period of dispersed searching by up to 14 librarians at six locations, Massachusetts Institute of Technology centralized its online searching and finds that the new arrangement is more efficient and more cost effective as well as better able to accommodate interdisciplinary research. In addition, according to MIT, the users benefit from superior searches, and appreciate the convenience of "one stop shopping."

---

[1] The University of Toronto and University of California at San Diego, for instance.

TABLE 6-1: REFERRAL SHEET

UNIVERSITY LIBRARY, STATE UNIVERSITY AT ALBANY

A COMPUTER PRODUCED BIBLIOGRAPHY FROM THE INFORM DATA BASE

When reading your printout you will notice that each INFORM reference consists of several labeled papargaphs of information:

AN   Abstract number

AU   Author/s

TI   Title

SO   Source

CD   ABI journal code

YR   Publication year

AB   Abstract

DATA BASE DESCRIPTION

The INFORM data base contains full bibliographic citations and abstracts from about 250 primary management and administrative journals. It contains over 30,000 citations from 1971 to the present. It is updated monthly. There is no printed index which corresponds to this data base.

LOCATING MATERIALS

Check the card catalog to locate books or periodical titles. Materials not owned by the Library may generally be ordered through Interlibrary Loan.

The librarians at the reference desk will be glad to assist you in reading your printout or locating materials.

CURRENT AWARENESS SERVICE

If you wish, you may request that a monthly update of your profile of interests be sent to you automatically. To begin this service, please phone the Information Retrieval Section (457-5272) for an appointment.

EVALUATION

We hope the results of this computer search will help meet your information needs. If the bibliography is not satisfactory for any reason, please contact the search department so that the retrieval failure may be evaluated and the search revised and reprocessed if necessary.

The days and hours during which online services will be available must also be decided upon. Here again, policies and practices vary rather widely from one library to the next. Generally, a conventional, five-day week seems to be preferred, with the service being available for a significant number of hours each day. Academic libraries with a tradition of providing evening and weekend service to their patrons, are likely to be under some pressure to extend the practice to the provision of online services. For example, the University of Kentucky, which normally offers online service from 8 A.M. to 5 P.M. Monday to Friday, also will search in the evening when one of its qualified people is on hand.

Increasingly, libraries are adopting the requirement that library patrons make advance appointments for interviews and search strategy negotiating sessions (e.g., UCLA and other campuses of the University of California). These permit both the patron and the information services librarian to schedule the event, to prepare for it, and to concentrate entirely on getting the most out of it. Appointments also facilitate scheduling access to the computer terminal, eliminate interruptions, peak loads, and waiting in line, and put the service on a more businesslike, professional basis.

SEARCH REQUEST FORMS

Less common, but equally well advised, is the requirement that the user complete and submit a search request form well in advance of the interview. This gives the information services librarian time to examine the request, make some preliminary strategic search decisions, assemble potentially helpful print materials, and sharply focus the interview from the outset. The result is a shorter negotiating session and more efficient service to the patron. The following pages show typical search request forms used at Princeton, at Stanford University, and at two campuses of the University of California. Like others throughout the country, these vary considerably in the amount of detail called for or encouraged.

SHOULD RESEARCHERS BE PRESENT?

Some years ago, there was considerable discussion, and a wide difference of opinion, on whether librarians or the ultimate seekers of information should conduct online lit-

TABLE 6-2: SEARCH FORM, PRINCETON

Princeton University
Reference Retrieval Service

Name (Requester)_____ Status_____ Dept._____

Appointment Date_____ Time_____ Account Number_____

Short Title_____

Completing this form prior to your appointment will increase the efficiency of PURRS service during your appointment and will probably lower the cost of service to you.

1. Please give in your own words a _narrative_ descriptive of the problem to be searched. Be specific, define _phrases_ with special meaning. Append a list to your narrative of any synonyms, closely-related phrases, and alternate spellings. Please indicate if any words or phrases have a special use that you wish to exclude. Use scientific and technical as well as common vocabulary.

_____
_____
_____
_____
_____
_____
_____
_____
_____
_____
_____
_____
_____

2. Unless already stated, please indicate any models, end uses, or applications that would be helpful in retrieving useful references for your problem.

_____
_____

Search Request (cont)

Name:_____

3. Please state any topics related to (or applications of, or views of, or approaches to) your specific problem that are not of interest if you wish to exclude retrieving citations to any documents on such topics.

_____

_____

4. Please give a title to your problem.

_____

5. Please list two or three of the most important authors (and/or organizations) publishing on your topic; complete names, if known, are helpful. Please indicate if you wish to exclude documents by any of these (or other) authors or organizations because of prior familiarity with their publications.

_____

_____

_____

6. Please list two or three of the most important journals covering your problem. Please indicate if you wish to retrieve references to documents from only these journals. Please indicate if you wish not to retrieve references to documents from any particular journal, perhaps because you personally receive the journal.

_____

_____

_____

_____

7. Do you wish either to retrieve or not retrieve references to documents written in a particular language?_____Does not matter_____Retrieve English only_____Retrieve only in _____Do not retrieve in_____

8. Do you wish to limit the search to a particular time span?_____Does not matter_____Retrieve 1975/ only_____Retrieve 1974/_____Other_____

9. Approximately how many citations would you expect?_____

10. Please list the complete citations to two or three of the most useful articles on your search topic. (It may be helpful to bring these articles to your appointment.)

_____

_____

_____

TABLE 6-3: STANFORD LIBRARIES
COMPUTER SEARCH SERVICE

Library Use Only*********
1. Search No._____
2. Library_____
3. Accepted_____
4. Searched by:_____
5. Data Bases_____

6. Name_____

7. Department_____

8. Mail Address (if different from above)
   _____

9. Home Phone: _____ 9a. Business Phone: _____

10. User: ___Faculty, ___Grad. Student (_____Ph.D), ____Staff
    ____Undergraduate, ____Other Stanford, ____Affiliated:_____

11. SEARCH TOPIC: Describe the subject/topic you want searched. Please state your description in prose. Here is an example: Citations that deal with the effects of any mutation on the eye color of the fruit fly (Drosophila melanogaster)."

12. KEYWORDS: List key terms, phrases or concepts that describe your topic or research. Give synonyms and spelling variations. Specify terms you do NOT want used in retrieving items.

13. SAMPLE CITATIONS: List 2 or 3 citations on your topic, if known or easily available.
    _____

14. LANGUAGES: _____English only. _____Any language. Languages in addition to English_____

15. RANGE OF YEARS WANTED : _____All years available, _____No items before 19_____.

16. ABSTRACTS NEEDED (if present in file searched) _____yes. _____no.

17. SCOPE OF SEARCH: Check the kind of search you want.

_____COMPREHENSIVE: In which an attempt will be made to retrieve the maximum number of items with the possibility that there may be a relatively high percentage of non-useful items.

_____LIMITED: In which an attempt will be made to retrieve a minimum acceptable number of items with the possibility a number of items that would be in a comprehensive search will not be retrieved.

18. FEE LIMIT: Give the approximate amount acceptable as a maximum fee. This will guide the searcher in the selection of data bases and in determining the scope of the search.

$_____

PLEASE NOTE: THE FEE PAYS FOR A SEARCH. IT IS POSSIBLE THAT NO RELEVANT CITATIONS WILL BE FOUND.

19. DEADLINE: State the latest date beyond which the search will not be useful to you.

NOT USEFUL AFTER_____

20. AUTHORIZATION: I authorize the library to perform the search described above and agree to the charges incurred in doing the search. Payment will be made by:

_____Check, _____Interdepartmental fund transfer, _____Cash

Signature_____   Date_____

CS-2(Rev.1 9/76)

Reprinted courtesy of Stanford University.

TABLE 6-4: SEARCH FORM, UCLA

UNIVERSITY OF CALIFORNIA THE UNIVERSITY LIBRARIES
UNIVERSITY-WIDE LIBRARY AUTOMATION PROGRAM CENTER FOR INFORMATION SERVICES (UCLA)

SEARCH REQUEST

Patron name_____ Date_____

Department_____ Tel._____ Status

Campus address_____ __UC Faculty
 __UC Graduate Student
(or address if non-UC)_____ __UC Undergraduate Student
 __UC Administration
City, state, zip_____ __UC Staff
 __Non-UC

****

Short title search _____

Please describe as fully as possible the subject in which you are interested. Be specific and define terms which have special meaning in the context of your request. Where appropriate, include alternate names for chemical and biological substances or compounds, common and scientific names of biological species, and names or descriptive terms for specific methods or techniques used in your research.

Important terms (and synonyms)...............or special uses you wish to exclude:

Please return this form to:

If there are authors or corporate authors whose writing is always of interest and should be included in the search, please list names as completely as possible. (For citation searching, please give complete bibliographic references. Attach extra pages if necessary.)

Please list two or three recent references of special interest to you in relation to this search.

What type of search do you need? (Check all applicable)
____RETROSPECTIVE - looking back over the available years of the data base
____CURRENT AWARENESS - looking forward to future issues of the data base

____BROAD - a fairly long list, missing few relevant references but probably including many non-relevant items.
____NARROW - a relatively short list containing most relevant items with the possibility that some relevant items will be missed.

QUALIFICATIONS. PLEASE NOTE THAT NOT ALL OF THE FOLLOWING ARE RETRIEVABLE ON EVERY DATA BASE!
 If appropriate to your search topic and/or data base(s) to be searched, please indicate qualifications desired:
Category: ___Human ___Animal(specify)_____ ___Male ___Female
Age:___0-1mo. ___1-23mo. ___2-5yrs. ___6-12 ___13-18 ___19-44 ___45-64 ___65-
School level: ___Primary ___Elementary ___Junior High ___High School
       ___Junior College ___College or University ___Adult education
Geographic:_____
Dates: What is the earliest year that references will be useful to you?_____
       (References from some data bases may go back to 1964 or 1966)
Language: ___English only ___Any language ___Other (specify) _____
****

Have you used this search service before?___Have you used another computer search service?___

How did you hear about this service? ___Librarian ___Student ___Professor/Advisor
 ___Class announcement ___Brochure ___Bulletin board ___Other notice
Purpose of search: ___Dissertation/Master's thesis ___Research ___Term paper/project
 ___Class related assignment ___Other _____
****

TABLE 6-5: SEARCH FORM, UNIVERSITY OF CALIFORNIA, IRVINE

Return to: Attn: Information Retrieval
            Physical Sciences Library
            P.O. Box 19557
            University of California, Irvine 92713

Or
Call: (714) 833-7237, Vincent Caccese

Date: _____

Requester: Please fill out items 1 - 8

1. Name (Please Print) _____

2. Position/Student Year _____ Telephone _____
                                                 (Area Code) Number
3. Department/Organization _____

    Mailing Address: _____

    _____

4. Please describe the subject in which you are interested and on which you want references. Be specific, and define terms which have special meaning in your request. If certain facets of the subject are not of interest to you, explicitly state that they are to be excluded.

5. List the important terms and synonyms or special uses you wish to exclude:

    Terms   Synonyms   Excluded Uses

    _____
    _____
    _____
    _____
    _____

6. List two references in your area of interest which you have found useful:

    _____
    _____
    _____
    _____

7. List any particular authors whose writing always is of interest to you:

8. Do you wish to receive references to documents written in:

English only _____ Any Language _____ Other (specify) _____

Date _____

Title of Search _____

BILLING

UCI _____

NOT UCI _____

Data bases and system to be searched: Rate/Min. $/Off-Line Hits

_____
_____
_____
_____
_____

Maximum $ _____

User's Authorization _____

Charge U.C. Account _____

To be filled out by analyst

File Name:_____	File Name:_____	File Name:_____
Date Run:_____	Date Run:_____	Date Run:_____
Log Off:_____	Log Off:_____	Log Off:_____
Log On:_____	Log On:_____	Log On:_____
Minutes:_____	Minutes:_____	Minutes:_____
Connect Cost:_____	Connect Cost:_____	Connect Cost:_____
Citations Off-Line:___	Citations Off-Line:___	Citations Off-Line:___
Total:_____	Total:_____	Total:_____

Search Formulation Time: Search Formulation Time: Search Formulation Time:
_____   _____   _____

DATA BASES AVAILABLE (10/1/76)

Please ask for descriptions of the following data bases as well as for current pricing.

DATA BASE NAME	SYSTEM /(FILE NO.)
ABI/INFORM (Management)	Dialog (15), SDC
Agricola (CAIN) (Agric., Botany, Entomol.)	Dialog (10), SDC
AIM/ARM (Instructional materials)	Dialog (9)
America: History & Life	Dialog (38)
ASI (Statistical)	SDC
BIOSIS (Bio. Abst. & Bio. Research)	Dialog (5), SDC
Cancerline	Elhill
Chemcon (Chemical Abst. 1972-)	Dialog (3), SDC
Chem 70/71 (Chemical Abst. 1970-71)	Dialog (2), SDC
Chemical Industry Notes	Dialog (19), SDC
CIS (Congressional hearings etc.)	SDC
Compendex (Engineering index)	Dialog (8), SDC
Computers & Control Abst.	Dialog (13)
CRecord (Congressional Record)	SDC
Dissertation Abstracts Index	Dialog (35), SDC
EIS (Industrial Plants Stats.)	Dialog (22)
Electrical Engr. Abst.	Dialog (13)
Energyline	Dialog (40)
Enviroline	Dialog (40), SDC
ERIC (Education)	Dialog (1), SDC, CIS
Exceptional Child Abst.	Dialog (4)
Foundation Directory	Dialog (26)
Foundation Grants	Dialog (27)
Georef (Geology)	SDC
Historical Abst.	Dialog (39)
Inform (Management)	Dialog (15), SDC
ISMEC (Mech. Engr.)	Dialog (14)
Language/Language Behavior Abst.	Dialog (?)
Medline 1966-	Elhill
Metals Abstracts	Dialog (32)
Meteorological Abst.	Dialog (29)
NTIS	Dialog (6), SDC
Oceanic Abst.	Dialog (28)
Paper Chemistry	SDC
P/E (Petroleum/Energy)	SDC
Pharmaceutical News Index	Dialog (42), SDC
Physics Abstracts	Dialog (12)
Pollution	Dialog (40), SDC
Predicasts (Marketing)	Dialog (16-21)
Psychological Abstracts	Dialog (11)
Scisearch (Science Citation Index)	Dialog (34)
Socscisearch (Social Science Citation Index)	Dialog (7)
SSIE (Research In Progess)	SDC
Toxline (Toxicology)	Elhill
Tulsa (Energy)	SDC
World Aluminum Abst.	Dialog (33)

erature searches. Those contending that the user of the information should conduct the searches directly pointed out that subject expertise is needed for effective searching.

The other camp contended that computer-readable bases are merely electronic counterparts of printed services familiar to reference librarians; and that in any case, most scientists and scholars have neither the time nor the inclination to master the intricacies of interactive online searching.

Experience since has settled the issue, for the time being at least, in favor of reference librarians acting as intermediaries between the user and the data base. (An interesting departure is The Science Information Service of The Warner Lambert/Parke Davis Pharmaceutical Research Division in Ann Arbor, MI, where all six science information specialists are chemists or biologists, not librarians, per se.)

There are scattered instances of end users directly performing their own searches on terminals located in the office or laboratory, and other instances in which end users conduct searches themselves on library terminals while an information services librarian makes his or her expertise available when needed or on request. The operating norm, however, is for the search requester to make his or her needs known to an information services librarian, who then formulates and conducts the search.

The brevity and heuristic nature of online searching, however, do make it feasible -- and even desirable -- to have the end user present during the actual search. With the user present, and "looking over the shoulder," as it were, of the search librarian at the terminal, the team can bring to bear the mutually supporting powers of the librarian's reference and computer searching expertise, and the user's in-depth command of the subject. An incidental benefit of this arrangement seems to be that users who are present during the actual search tend to be more satisfied with the results, and more convinced that the search was comprehensive and ably carried out, than are users who simply delegate the search to be performed in their absence.[1]

To be sure, there are some disadvantages in having the user present during the search. Chief among these is the problem of scheduling a search when both the searcher and the user can be present. A second difficulty is that the

---

[1] Ellen Pearson of the University of Guelph and Sara Knapp of SUNY-Albany both mention this factor.

actual search itself tends to be longer when the end user is present. Not all of this additional connect time, and therefore cost, is related to getting an objectively more effective search.

Too often, particularly when a packaged or standard search is being performed for a fixed amount of money, a user will spot a citation of only marginal relevance to the search then underway, that deals with, or touches upon, another topic of interest to the user. He will then want to pursue other citations of that sort before getting back to the central investigation. This incidental mini-search may lead to another sidetrack exploration, which may in turn trigger still another, and so forth. Unless the information services librarian quickly detects what's happening and insists on a more disciplined search, this kind of browsing can prove very expensive.

Solutions to the first problem, in addition to requiring that an appointment be made well in advance, might include accommodating walk-in clients during certain scheduled hours, or having the searcher stay in contact with the user by telephone during the conduct of the search. Both ploys are used by Bell Laboratories, Murray Hill, NJ, and by the University of Kentucky (Lexington), among others. A common solution to the second problem is to invite, or permit, end users to be present at the terminal only during custom or specialized searches of such complexity that the user would have important contributions to make while the searcher is online. This is the approach taken at the Van Pelt Library at the University of Pennsylvania in Philadelphia, for instance. Simple, or standard searches that are performed for a fixed fee are conducted by the search specialist without the user present.

Some provision must also be made for the important postsearch activities, both of the user and of the information services librarian. At minimum, arrangements have to be made for the user to receive a printout of the citations retrieved in the search. Those printed online can, of course, be picked up at once if the user is present during the search itself, but online printing is relatively expensive. Further, in most cases, a list of citations that are subsequently printed offline will be more extensive, and more likely to include abstracts.

These offline printouts can be sent directly to the library patron, but there may be merit in having them sent, instead, to the librarian who conducted the search. This way, the searcher can review the citations in terms of their recall, relevance, and precision, and perhaps add further citations uncovered by a parallel search of print media. In addition, citations that appear redundant or not appropriate can be deleted, and possibly the entire output can be organized or repackaged to make it more useful.

Many librarians also prefer to conduct a post-search interview with the end user, during which they mutually assess and evaluate the results of the search, consider rerunning the search if it was unsuccessful, and decide on how best to go about acquiring full-text copies of the documents deemed to be most useful.

Naturally, as choices and decisions are made with regard to the various aspects of establishing modes of operation and service procedure, they will have to be formalized and reduced to writing. However, ample provision should be made to keep things flexible. The field of online reference services is highly dynamic. As libraries gain experience at it, they will want to make changes in the scope of services, and in the forms and procedures for providing them.

7
Marketing and Promotion

With the possible exception of users' fees, no aspect of online bibliographic reference services is more alien to librarians than the need to actively promote and market these services. Nevertheless, experience invariably confirms that sustained and aggressive promotion is essential. Without it, the likelihood of attracting enough patronage to justify continuing the service approaches nil. Further, the service can only be of value if patrons take advantage of it; and, of course, they cannot take advantage of something they know nothing about.

The crux of the issue then, and the real objective of the promotional efforts that must be made is user education. Of course, educating library patrons with respect to the facilities and services available, is itself rather foreign to the traditions and practices of most libraries. Characteristically, libraries and librarians alike have been content to assume a passive, almost deferential, role with regard to library patrons, and to virtually ignore non-users, even though the result may be only limited and sporadic use of the libraries' resources.

This pattern is compounded by the predominantly formal atmosphere of the library itself, and by the cool and reserved posture of many librarians. The result creates in the minds of too many potential users an impression of the library as proprietary territory whose scope, dimensions, and promise are only dimly understood. However eager to serve and be helpful librarians may be (once a patron has taken the initiative and broken the ice) too many are content to rely on pamphlets and word of mouth among patrons to make the world aware of the full scope of services available.

NEED FOR PROMOTION OF ONLINE SERVICES

Particularly in the case of online reference services, however, which are comparatively new and a startling departure from traditional library offerings, potential users are not only understandably ignorant of the services, but in most cases have no reason to suspect that they might exist. Accordingly, the library must take the educational initiative. The effort can be restrained or flamboyant, narrowly focused or energetically broadcast, but it must be made. Moreover, it must be sustained more or less indefinitely.

The effort should begin with some basic market research and some strategic marketing decisions. The market research consists of specifically identifying and locating the potential user groups who can most benefit from the service and are most likely to be attracted to it. Without a fairly clear idea of who will be using the services, the library will be unable to relate its promotional literature and demonstrations to the perceived reference needs of potential users.

Fortunately, in any well thought out program the location, size, and general nature of the potential user population will have been identified during the exploratory stages leading up to the decision to institute online reference services. Thus, it remains only to isolate this clientele in more specific terms.

One marketing decision to be made early is whether to launch a broad-gauged publicity blitzkrieg at the outset, in hopes of attracting maximum attention and some vanguard users from each of the target populations, or whether to carefully restrict the initial promotion to a single user group with high potential. The advantage of the latter approach is that it is less costly, affords the library the opportunity to gain promotional experience from a limited effort before undertaking something more ambitious, and limits the incremental work load imposed on the library by the new online patrons.

The latter consideration is especially important for libraries that initiate online reference services without expanding the library staff. In addition, a controlled buildup of patronage permits the information services librarians to gain search experience and proficiency before they are required to cope with substantial demand for their services. Finally, a carefully focused appeal to a particular clientele permits a library with limited resources to initiate online searching with only one or a few data bases. Subsequently, the library can expand both its offerings and the clientele it serves.

If this strategy is undertaken, of course, it is extremely important that the limited initial offerings be publicized only to those who can take advantage of them. Potential patrons who hear about the online reference services incidentally, and arrive at the library with search assignments that cannot be accommodated on the data bases then available, are likely to feel disappointed and deprived -- and to communicate their frustration to other potential users. Moreover, they may put the library under pressure to expand the scope of its online offerings more rapidly than is planned or advisable.

The alternative decision -- to broadcast the availability of online reference services across a large variety of data bases in the hope of quickly attracting a substantial cadre of early users -- carries with it certain hazards of its own. One is that the effort might be too successful, inundating the service with demand levels that cannot be accommodated comfortably. Dallas Public Library triggered a related problem when it announced, with great public ballyhoo, that it had The New York Times Information Bank online. The public rushed in, convinced that NYTIB was some sort of electronic encyclopedia. Disillusioning them created a durable black eye for the library.

A second hazard is that unless adequate provision has been made in the start-up budget for the cost of promoting and demonstrating the new services, a library can find itself in a "Catch 22" situation: on the one hand, it is under the gun to attract the maximum number of new users, through demonstrations and publicity; on the other hand, it is unable to afford to sustain the effort necessary to do so.

A third hazard is that users who respond to the initial promotional efforts but cannot be promptly accommodated, owing to a logjam of demand, will be frustrated and disgruntled.[1] The risk of creating a core of disappointed potential users is very great, because word-of-mouth publicity is far and away the most powerful medium available. Too many dissatisfied customers can ultimately defeat even an expensive promotional campaign.

WHAT MARKET TO GO AFTER

Another strategic marketing decision that must be made early is that of market segmentation, that is, dividing the total, heterogeneous market for online reference services into homogenous segments with relatively common needs and interests.

---

[1] Soon after offering online services in 1973, SUNY at Albany had a backlog of 150 search requests.

For example, a university library might partition its market along departmental lines (psychology, chemistry, biology, economics, etc.), or according to academic status (faculty, graduate students, undergraduates, off-campus users). Such differentiators can also be combined to produce, for instance, "life sciences faculty" as one market segment and "undergraduate physics students" as another.

A given market segment will be interested in access to certain data bases while having no use for others. One market segment may require searches of a depth and chronological scope that would never be required by a member of a different one. To dramatize the point, consider the differing needs of a career medical researcher on the one hand, and, on the other, an undergraduate education major in the throes of preparing an overdue term paper.

The purpose of market segmentation, of course, is to permit the libraries' promotional efforts to be tailored exactly to the needs of each particular group being addressed. Another gross, but nonetheless functional, form of market segmentation is to divide the total community, or population, served by the library into two groups: those who do and those who do not take advantage of the traditional library facilities. Again, the marketing approach taken to the two groups would differ. The library will have established some rapport and credibility with the former group, so promotional efforts can build on this base with emphasis on the particular user benefits associated with the new online reference services.

The latter, and larger, group of potential users must be approached in a different way, with emphasis, perhaps, on the library itself as an intellectual resource to be called upon, and with online services being presented as only one of a number of other non-print holdings and services, including sound recording, films, and the like.

It may well be that many of the potential users within the non-patron category have been ignoring the library in the past because of dissatisfaction with the resources that they perceived of as being available. For these people, the speed, convenience, and personalized service available in connection with online reference services may provide what they found missing in the past.

With both groups, of course, the library must still demonstrate the ability of online services to meet specific needs of the patrons who try them.

MARKETING TACTICS

Once these strategic marketing decisions have been made -- what services to offer initially, and for what groups -- those concerned with promoting online reference services can address themselves to the tactical measures that might prove most effective. One useful ploy is to identify the few key personnel or "thought leaders" within a given user group, and to concentrate on persuading these individuals to try the online reference services. Commonly, such incentives as artificially low -- or even no -- fee searches are employed to make it easier for these bellwether accounts to agree to trial searches.[1]

Examples of such key personnel would include department heads, project leaders, prestigious scientists, and "information gatekeepers," members of the so-called invisible colleges that seem to exist in virtually all professional fields. These are the individuals to whom others in the field turn for information, and who play a central role in the sometimes elaborate but informal information and communications networks through which colleagues in an institution, or specialists within a particular field, exchange information -- frequently by telephone.

The objective of inducing these leaders to utilize the new online reference services, of course, is both to create a record of successful searches for demanding individuals, resulting in at least their implied, if not actively expressed, endorsement of the service; and to make active users out of a cadre of individuals in a strong position to influence others.

Tactical alternatives range from offering free, or very low cost, sample searches to all comers, to pressing a vigorous publicity and educational campaign directed either at a target user group or at the client community at large. While some libraries have successfully used the telephone for this purpose, Betty Miller and David Mindel of Calspan Corp. caution that phone solicitors must be sure they are talking to key people. "Otherwise," they say, "you may spend a good hour fascinating a clerk, secretary etc." and never reach the decision-makers.

---

[1] The University of California at Berkeley has offered free trial searches to key faculty members, including demonstrating the system in their classes.

Most library promotion relies instead, or at least primarily, on the various traditional print media available. Examples include:

. Flyers that are widely distributed to potential users, announcing the online search service and offering low cost trials;

. Publicity releases;

. Brochures describing the online services and the various data bases available;

. Price lists;

. Posters and bulletin board announcements;

. Book marks and other favors and handouts;

. Formal advertisements, announcements, and articles in appropriate magazines, papers, and house organs;

. Printed collections of typical questions asked about the service, along with their answers;

. Newsletters;

. Direct mail pieces;

. Reminders to be enclosed with payroll checks, service invoices, and the like.

Most of these promotional materials can be generated at low cost on local copying or duplicating facilities; all that is required is the imagination to create them. One example is the fairly comprehensive handbook "Instructional Resources" distributed by the Center for Educational Development in the Walter Library at the University of Minnesota. An excerpt of this handbook, dealing specifically with computer-based bibliographic search services, is shown on the following pages.

Another effective and very low cost tactic using print media is to make use of the various catalogs, guidebooks, handbooks, and the like that are prepared and distributed by the institution in any case. Each such publication can carry a descriptive paragraph or two announcing, and sketching in the general outlines of, the online reference services available through the library. Academic libraries find this promotional

TABLE 7-1 INSTRUCTIONAL RESOURCES AT

THE UNIVERSITY OF MINNESOTA

Excerpts from the Instructional Resources Handbook produced by the Center for Educational Development, 317 Walter Library, Minneapolis, MN 55455, James H. Werntz, Jr. Director (Third Edition).

*   *   *

LIBRARY SEARCH SERVICES

Beyond the regular reference services available in all library units, there is a specialized program which provides, on a fee basis, in-depth bibliographic searching:

> INFORM, a service in Wilson Library (373-5938, Judy Wells) will provide information to any patron, on or off campus, to whatever depth is required. Examples of services available are compilations of bibliographies, extensive literature and information source surveys, publication of guides to the literature, compilation of statistics, preparation of reference guides or handbooks on particular industries or subjects, and current awareness programs.

Also available, on a fee basis, are a number of computer data base search services. Currently available are the following:

In the Bio-Medical Library (373-7233, Gertrude Foreman):

> MEDLINE or MEDLARS, a computer-based service with direct telecommunications access to the Index Medicus bibliographic data base, covers approximately 2,700 medical, nursing, dental, and life science journals indexed by the National Library of Medicine from 1966 to the present. In addition, there are other data bases covering CANCER, EPILEPSY, CHEMLINE, and AV-LINE.

> SDILINE, a current awareness service from the MEDLARS data base, provides a monthly update of citations on a subject of choice. SDILINE covers the most recent indexing from the National Library of Medicine and is available one month before publication of the printed monthly *Index Medicus*.

> TOXLINE is an extensive collection of computerized toxicology journal references, including toxicity studies, environmental studies, and drug reactions. The data base contains: *Chemical-Biological Activities,* 1965 to date; *Abstract of Health Effects of Environmental Pollutants,* 1972 to date; *International Pharmaceutical Abstracts,* 1970 to date; *Toxicity Bibliography,* 1968 to date; and *Health Aspects of Pesticides Abstract Bulletin,* 1966 to date.

In the Business Reference Service (373-4109, Judy Wells):

   INFORM, produced by Abstracted Business Information, Inc., provides comprehensive coverage of the literature in such areas as banking, finance, insurance, management, economics, statistics, business law, and marketing. Major feature articles are abstracted from more than 280 journals. Coverage is from 1971 to the present.

In the Chemistry Library (373-2375, Beverly Lee):

   CHEMCON (Chemical Abstracts Condensates), produced by Chemical Abstracts Service, is a weekly current awareness service that provides information from the corresponding issues of Chemical Abstracts. Coverage is from 1970 to the present.

In the Education Library (373-3841, Celia Ellingson):

   ERIC (Educational Resources Information Center), the educational data base maintained by the U.S. National Institute of Education, covers reports and periodical literature in education-related fields from 1966 to the present. Microfiche copies of the reports in the file are available at a nominal cost.

   AIM/ARM (Abstracts of Instructional Material/Abstracts of Research Materials) lists 7000 abstracts of instructional and research materials, indexed by the Center for Vocational and Technical Education, Ohio State University.

   EXCEPTIONAL CHILDREN ABSTRACTS includes 12,000 abstracts of material of particular interest in this field.

   PSYCH ABSTRACTS lists more than 125,000 abstracts to journal articles in psychology dating from 1967 indexed by the Americal Psychological Association.

In the Engineering Library (373-2957, Crystal Clift):

   COMPENDEX, produced by *Engineering Index,* is a data base corresponding to the monthly issues of *Engineering Index Monthly.* AI examines over 3,500 journals and other types of publications, including proceedings of conferences, to provide world-wide coverage in all disciplines of engineering from 1970 to the present.

   GEOREF (Geological Reference File), produced by the American Geological Institute, provides world-wide coverage of the geosciences including economic geology, geochemistry, marine geology, solid-earth geophysics, and engineering-environmental geology. The data base includes 3,000 journals and coverage of conferences, symposia, and major monograhps from 1967 to the present.

* * *

ploy especially useful in such documents as thesis-preparation booklets and the handbooks or guidebooks made available to help grant applicants. In this fashion, potential users become aware of the online services at a time when they are especially interested in learning about the resources available to them; and, in time to incorporate their cost into the proposed budget for the contemplated research project. A valuable promotional element can also be found in the efforts of some libraries to integrate online and conventional bibliographic search tools. For instance, the University of Kentucky tags appropriate printed indexes with a prominent question: "Do you know that this index can be searched online?" Similarly the State University of New York at Albany lists in its online services brochure the call numbers of printed counterparts of each available data base.

Another very popular promotional gambit is the conduct of demonstration searches before groups of influential and interested potential users of the service. Acknowledging the convincing impact of such sample searches, the principal retrieval service vendors cooperate by making a limited number of such searches available at very low cost. Dartmouth typically offers one or two demonstrations in the Fall, and starting this year, graduate engineering students will be required to perform a literature search as part of their thesis or dissertation preparation. Many will very likely opt to have the search conducted online (the maximum charge is $15.00 per search). Particularly effective is the tactic of conducting an online search in an area of immediate interest to one of the witnesses of the demonstration. In fact, these are so intriguing and convincing that it's a good idea to fix some arbitrary limits -- such as 10 citations printed online, or perhaps five input descriptors -- in order to avoid inadvertent abuse of the demonstration privilege. The University of California at Berkeley, for one, suggests that 10 citations printed online is ample for a demonstration.

Other helpful promotional techniques include making announcements and presentations at important meetings such as graduate student orientations; brief seminars and speeches to appropriate groups; and direct, one-to-one contact with department chairmen, department librarians, and other important potential users of the online reference services.

A growing number of libraries, including that of Calspan Corp. (formerly Cornell Aeronautical Laboratory) -- one of the few company libraries that offer online services to outsiders -- have gone a step further, by commissioning or preparing audio-visual presentations that dramatize their marketing efforts. Kris Brooks of Oregon State University uses slides and a script for her one-hour presentations, each of which is tailored to suit the prospects she is addressing. She finds this much more productive than giving free demonstrations, and its a great deal less expensive and more versatile. It would seem appropriate for the principal data base and retrieval service vendors to prepare introductory audio-visual packages describing their services in general terms, but as of this writing none has seen fit to do so. This is probably because the bulk of their customers to date have been special and research libraries, which, with a "captive" and relatively stable clientele, are characteristically not faced with as intense and pervasive an educational task as are academic libraries.

This is not at all to say that special libraries can entirely avoid the need to promote online services, however. Several years ago Lawrence, Weil and Graham described their initial internal marketing effort as follows: "When we were ready, the first step in our full-fledged campaign was a series of demonstrations for research division managers. Each demonstration was introduced with a brief definition of on-line, interactive searching, a mention of available (and soon to be available) information bases, and an estimate of average costs. Then a single on-line search was made on an appropriate subject (pretested as being relevant and with 'good' answers). After that, we encouraged 'live' questions -- which often produced useful results on the spot.

"The other two steps in our publicity effort were the publication of a feature article in the company newspaper and a word-of-mouth campaign both by the information staff and enthusiastic researchers. Whether people came to try the Library's new 'toy' or to get some of those good (and fast) search results, they usually went away pleased -- and they told others. More than for almost any of our information programs, word-of-mouth publicity has been a major factor in the success of this program."[1]

IMPORTANCE OF WORD-OF-MOUTH

This express recognition of the overriding importance of word-of-mouth publicity to the successful implementation and

---

[1] Barbara Lawrence, Ben H. Weil, Margaret H. Graham, "Making On-line Search Available in an Industrial Environment," Journal of The American Society for Information Science, November/December 1974.

maintenance of online bibliographic reference services underlines one final, but extremely important, promotional consideration: the experiences and impressions that the users of online reference services have, and exchange with one another, can by themselves make or break the entire undertaking virtually regardless of any other factor in the equation. As Donald Hawkins of Bell Labs noted in an interview, "Word-of-mouth promotion is the best there is."

If the services performed are perceived as being successful and helpful, they will be talked up and demand for the continued service will grow. If the users are disappointed with the results achieved, or feel that the results are not cost effective, they will not only stop using the service, but will talk it down among their associates, and the service in time is doomed.

Accordingly, it is of the first importance that the searchers be well trained and that the searches themselves produce useful results, the value of which clearly exceeds their cost. Every member of the online searching staff who comes in direct contact with users and potential users must accept, as among his or her important responsibilities, the need to promote the use and benefits of these services.

Clearly, this orientation and responsibility are particularly important in the case of the information services librarians who function as the intermediaries between the patrons of the service and the system itself. They must be personable, enthusiastic, assertively helpful, and communicative, as well as merely competent. They must, in short, be market-oriented, and the market is the user they are serving.

RESPONSIBILITY FOR MARKETING AND PROMOTION

Beyond the general responsibility on the part of searchers to promote the service they are offering, it is probably advisable in most libraries to have someone specifically responsible for marketing and promotion. Since most search staffs are small, this task will often fall to the unit supervisor -- as in Oregon State University or the Calspan Corp. Other libraries may have large enough staffs to be able to name someone as a promotion specialist. This is the person who will give talks or demonstrations, write promotional copy, and be able to field inquiries from potential users. Many, if not most, corporate libraries find that while initial promotion is important, the longer term problem is one of coping with spontaneous and sustained demand, without formal promotion. Academic and public libraries, however, experience a much heavier "turnover" of individual clients, so sustained promotion is imperative.

Having said all this, it would be naive to pretend that such activities will come easily, especially in a public or academic library setting. Vigorous marketing of a service for which the library is charging money smacks of commercialism, and many librarians will instinctively shy away from such endeavors. The head of the library, or the head of the reference department, must come to grips with this problem at the outset when online services are initiated. Because of the widespread feeling on the part of libraries engaged in online services that such services will not succeed without promotion, the library faces a difficult dilemma. It can offer a new service that can greatly improve the library's overall service to users -- at the cost of mounting a commercial sort of promotional campaign. Or it can maintain its traditional posture of avoiding marketing and promotion -- and by so doing prolong the length of time it takes for online services to "catch on" well enough to justify continuing them.

Next to the need to charge users, the promotional aspects of online services are the hardest for many libraries to swallow. Some would probably do well to recognize that, with present staff or present attitudes, they cannot effectively offer and promote such services themselves, and should simply refer patrons to other institutions. Others will recognize the obstacles, but decide that they should go ahead and work on changing the attitudes of their own professional staff members. In either case, administrators responsible for the decision must be clear in their own minds about what it entails, and able to spell out its ramifications for all concerned.

8
Management and Control

Many of the management and control considerations involved with the provision of online reference services are either implicit or explicit in the material already discussed. Examples include policy decisions with respect to the scope of services to be provided, the access times and locations of service, establishing a budget and financial controls, etc. Certain other aspects of the management picture, such as motivation, delegation, span of control, and the like, are part of managing any activity and therefore need no particular elaboration here.

SELECTING THE COORDINATOR

Nevertheless, a number of managerial concerns associated with providing online reference services remain to be addressed. One of the most important of these is that of selecting the individual who will be responsible for the undertaking. In most libraries this responsibility rests with the coordinator of online reference services.

While the specific duties assigned to this person vary somewhat from one library to the next, he or she is usually responsible for:

. Maintaining contact with the suppliers of retrieval systems and online data bases as well as with users;

. Training, scheduling and, in some cases, selecting the search staff;

. Conducting demonstrations and user education about the program;

. Publicity, marketing and promotion;

. Seeing that information services librarians stay abreast of the latest changes in data bases and search techniques;

. Coordinating the efforts of searchers operating at different locations;

. Keeping searchers supplied with forms, search aids, and the like;

. Compiling appropriate statistics, records, and reports;

. Monitoring and managing the service to assure that it meets its objectives.

At the University of California at San Diego, the coordinator's job description reads as follows:

"The coordinator shall report to the assistant librarian for public services, and shall be responsible for planning, instituting, coordinating and evaluating the library's computerized information services; serving as the library's liaison with vendors of information services; becoming thoroughly familiar with the Medline, DIALOG and ORBIT systems and serving as the resource person for librarian searchers; coordinating and supervising the training of librarians in the use of computerized information systems; publicizing the search services so that users are attracted to the services; and performing searches.

"Additional duties include formulating budgets and proposals and handling budgetary matters for the service; recommending appropriate policies to the public services librarian; contributing to the review process of those librarians who function full or part time as computerized literature searchers; supervising clerical staff assigned to the service; monitoring the use of the search systems to see that they are being effectively and efficiently utilized; initiating orders for appropriate supplies and equipment; developing appropriate forms and defining and collecting appropriate statistics; scheduling the use of available computer terminals; serving as a backup searcher for the service, so that the service is available in each library on a continuous basis."

The University of Rochester lists the responsibilities of the coordinator this way:

"Oversee the service, serve as the main person to answer questions concerning the service; develop and coordinate the publicity; coordinate demonstrations; conduct demonstrations; work with the searchers to provide guidance when necessary and be involved with the interviews with users when necessary; conduct or coordinate seminars on how to handle searches, and how to integrate computer and manual information sources; work closely with searchers to answer questions when necessary; may train new searchers; evaluate the addition of new data bases; arrange for the physical setup of the terminal area; compile statistics, including evaluation of searches; supervise accounting and budgetary procedures connected with data bases; write any necessary manuals and instructions; serve as the main library contact with non-university library groups in the area of computer data based services; keep up to date on computer searching activities in the information field; and collect and disseminate information on availability of off-line searching services."

At Michigan State University, the job is called "Coordinator of the Office of Computerized Information Services," and the job description includes the following characteristic duties:

1) Recruits participating librarians and develops appropriate training programs for the use of data base services;

2) Works with personnel in other library departments for utilization of data bases in internal library operations;

3) Schedules terminal use and searching interviews, and maintains appropriate records;

4) Conducts searches when participating librarians are not available, and on new data bases prior to arranging for assistance from participating librarians;

5) Makes recommendations to the assistant director for expansion of data base access and services;

6) Performs other duties as assigned.

Clearly, the person chosen as coordinator of the online reference services must possess all or most of the characteristics that are desirable in any information services librarian. In addition, he or she must possess strong leadership, organizational and administrative abilities, and be able to inspire the confidence of both the professional and the clerical staff being supervised. The ideal candidate should be an articulate, believable advocate of online services, sensitive to the importance of providing consistently high quality service on the one hand, and to maintaining efficient operations and sensible cost control on the other.

This is a key position that preferably should be filled very soon after the initial decision to provide online search services. It's also important to recognize that, in most cases, the candidates available will not include anyone who is clearly ideal on all, or even most counts, so that in any specific situation, the job must be structured to some extent around the talent available.

Running an online reference department is a very demanding job -- particularly during the start-up operation -- and accordingly, the responsibilities of the job should not be drawn with unrealistic breadth and sweep. For instance, while it may very well be important for the coordinator -- especially in a library of modest size -- to function as a backup searcher, he or she is not likely to do enough actual searching to maintain dazzling proficiency. No matter. Personally conducting searches is -- and ought to be -- a very incidental and occasional activity of the services coordinator. (In many libraries, of course, a single individual conducts the entire online operation, but services on this scale hardly call for a coordinator.)

Careful recordkeeping, on the other hand, is far from incidental, and it should receive early and sustained attention. Records of each search, including the date, the requester, data base or bases used, the number of citations retrieved, and the time spent online at the terminal, must be kept, not only to verify invoices from suppliers, but to permit management to make more informed scheduling decisions.

As a rule, a custom tailored, online search seems to take about one hour, divided approximately into thirds; one-third each being spent on pre-search interviews and strategy formulation, on active searching at the computer terminal, and in post-search activities such as reviewing and editing results.

In some libraries, however, searchers commonly spend up to an hour in post-search activities alone. In addition, the time needed for such activities as training, update reading, and more conventional reference duties vary not only from one library to the next, but from time to time within a given library. Accordingly, searches cannot be scheduled on the basis of fudged-figure averages drawn from the literature. They must be scheduled on the basis of what is actually happening in the library in question, and this can only be ascertained by maintaining careful records.

Records are also important as the basis for calculating broader measures of efficiency, effectiveness, and user satisfaction, such as the total elapsed time between a patron's initial request for a search and his receipt of the printed output bibliography.

A number of online reference services have established turnaround and quality goals, progress toward which is routinely monitored. For instance, a library may set a general limit of completing searches within two working days after acceptance of an order. Another example might be setting as a goal having the offline printout from a search available to the patron within seven working days.

Surprisingly few libraries make a disciplined attempt to monitor user satisfaction with their online reference services. A minimal effort would seem to be to ask library patrons to fill out some kind of an evaluation form when, or after, they pick up their search printouts. A simple form can be devised, asking the users to check boxes or write down the number of citations they found relevant (or irrelevant). One such form, hardly an ideal, but characteristic, is that used at the Ernest R. Bird Library at Syracuse University shown on the following page.

The users might also be asked to rate their satisfaction with the recall rate of the search and with the utility of the results. They might be asked if the search measured up to their expectations, and if not, in what specific ways it fell short. Each user should certainly be asked if he or she considers the search to be worth its out-of-pocket cost, and whether or not he or she intends to use the serv-

TABLE 8-1: EVALUATION FORM, SYRACUSE UNIVERSITY

Name _____ Date _____ Phone _____ Dep't. _____
Faculty ( ) Undergrad ( ) Grad ( ) Other _____

Have you used this ERIC computer-based service before? ( )Yes ( )No
Is your topic: (A) Funded research   (C) Dissertation related   (E) Course related
               (B) Dissertation Proposal (D) Literature Review   (F) Personal project
****
WE NEED THE FOLLOWING INFORMATION TO HELP US EVALUATE AND IMPROVE OUR SERVICE TO YOU. WHEN YOU HAVE RECEIVED AND USED YOUR PRINTOUT PLEASE REPLY TO THE QUESTIONS BELOW AND RETURN THE FORM USING THE CAMPUS MAIL BOX IN YOUR DEPT.
        SEND TO: ERIC COMPUTER-BASED SURVEY (PAA), 113 EUCLID AVE.

1. (a) Overall were you ( )satisfied ( )unsatisfied with the search results?
   (b) If time permitted would you do a revised search?   ( )Yes ( )No

2. Was the printout received: ( )Earlier than expected ( )In time for your purpose ( )Too late

3. Comment on availability of assistance

	Immediately	After some delay	None	Not desired
(a) Pre-search assistance (e.g. aid in formulating the search strategy, use of descriptors, generally in answering questions about the proposed search)				
(b) Post-search assistance (e.g. interpretation of the printout, location of articles, revised search if desired)				

4. Estimate the percentage of relevant citations from the printout. Using the scale below, mark an X on the line to show your estimate.

   0%   25   50   75   100%
              Percentage of Relevant Citations

5. How many citations were of no use? _____ In what ways didn't they apply:

6. Please appraise the following components of the complete ERIC service noting difficulty (#) or ease (*) of use. Sought assistance? Time of Day? Available?

	#	*	Comments		
RIE					
CIJE					
Thesaurus of ERIC descriptors					
Printout					
Locating ERIC Documents					
Locating Journals cited					
Microfiche readers					

ice again. Finally, the form should allow ample room for the user's own comments and suggestions or criticisms.

This sort of feedback puts no great burden on the users -- many of whom are likely to welcome the opportunity to express themselves -- and it can provide important insights into ways of improving the service. Moreover, simply expressing an interest in the user's viewpoint and evaluation in itself indicates an eagerness to please and be of service, and helps to project a businesslike, customer-oriented image.

Such feedback from patrons should, of course, find its way back to the searcher who served each one. The searchers, too, can also provide valuable, and in many ways more meaningful, evaluations of the success of each search that they conduct. Users can be well pleased with a search even when the search librarian is not. Finally, the coordinator can gain further insights by monitoring an occasional pre-search interview and assessing its success. Forms, such as the one on the following page, can help structure these quality assessments, and make them more consistent and more rapid. Similar forms could be devised to provide an assessment of searchers' online skills and post-search activities.

Such monitoring can only be done on a sampling basis, of course, and the focus must remain on the quality of the search itself. If the searcher feels that his or her personal performance is being monitored, tension, resentment, and overstriving are likely to result.

In evaluating searches, and in considering the evaluations made by users and others, it is important to recognize that some of the criteria used will necessarily be subjective, and that even the objective ones are subject to certain qualifications. It's conceivable that "low cost" might be the key ingredient to an undergraduate assessing the success of a search in connection with a term paper, whereas a "high degree of relevance" might be most important to a research scientist. And, "maximum recall" might top the list of a scholar, eager to discover if any rival has beaten him to a new idea for a research project, or one who is preparing an article that features a review of the literature.

Various libraries try to measure the efficiency with which their online services are being provided, and a number of different approaches are being tried. One interesting measure of search efficiency has been proposed by Eileen Hitchingham of Oakland University in Rochester, MI:

TABLE 8-2: THE PRE-SEARCH INTERVIEW: AN ASSESSMENT OF SUCCESS (ATHERTON)

<u>Success</u> means a search request was negotiated fully, with the search strategy formulated so as to retrieve mainly relevant citations with a minimum of false drops and with few relevant documents known to be in the data base missing from output.

<u>Analysis</u>:

There were conditions which could influence the success of this interview: (check any which apply)

<u>User was</u>:

___ 1. prepared for interview

___ 2. expressive of information needs

___ 3. asking too broad a question

___ 4. asking too narrow a question

___ 5. knowledgeable about subject area

___ 6. active participant in interview

___ 7. helpful in suggesting terms

___ 8. flexible participant in interview

___ 9. responsive to information specialist's suggestions

<u>Information Specialist was</u>:

___ 1. interested in user's need.

___ 2. able to probe most aspects of user's interests related to request.

___ 3. able to use aids adequately.

___ 4. able to explain system and data bases adequately.

___ 5. knowledgeable about subject.

___ 6. helpful in suggesting terms.

___ 7. helpful in suggesting strategies

___ 8. responsive to user's suggestions.

<u>Overall</u>: Interactive skills were:

___ very good ___ average
___ lacking

<u>Overall</u>: Interactive skills were:

___ very good ___ average
___ lacking

<u>Prediction</u>:

The interview was potentially successful: Yes___   No___   Can't Tell___

"From the user's viewpoint, a different measure of efficiency might be considered; actual cost (invoiced charges) per relevant citation in relation to recall. This value takes the cost of charges incurred for printing of irrelevant citations into account as well as terminal efficiency."

Such a measure would be expressed as x dollars, or y cents, per relevant citation at n% recall. It would be revealing and meaningful to the library and the patron alike, and it has the merit of demonstrating the folly of saving money by deliberately brief sessions at the terminal at the cost of extravagantly long offline printouts of citations, many of which are of no value.

The cost effectiveness of online reference services is virtually taken for granted at the libraries that offer them. One finding of the SDC survey by Wanger et al is that three out of four managers of online reference services consider them to be "more cost effective than manual searching." About the same ratio of active searchers agreed that online searching is "economical compared to manual searching."

Whether or not these opinions are justified is open to some question, because so few libraries have dependable comparative data. Furthermore, nearly all of the published accounts purporting to document cost effectiveness ignore or casually dismiss major component cost elements, particularly the cost of staff time and related overhead.[1] The cost effectiveness of any reference service is extremely hard to measure, although selected cost elements can be isolated and compared fairly readily.

Such measures, while interesting, must be kept in perspective, however. Online searching is by no means a complete substitute for manual searching. In any case, the objective of offering reference services -- online or otherwise -- is to meet the information needs of the library patrons, not simply to respond to queries with startling speed, or to generate bargain-basement bibliographies.

A related, but more appropriate pursuit, would be cost-benefit analysis. A useful methodology for achieving this has been developed by the Lower Pioneer Valley Regional Commission.[2] In the last analysis, though, the real touch-

---

[1] For a realistic study, see Collette and Price, op. cit.

[2] Final Report, Regional Information System: Feasibility Report, West Springfield, MA, 1973.

stone to user satisfaction is the utility of the results achieved by the online reference services. Search output need not be instantly available; it's enough that it be available on time to be useful. A search need not be cheap; it's enough that it be cheaper, all things considered, than alternative ways of acquiring the same information. From the patron's standpoint, convenience and effectiveness seem more important than search efficiency.

Such gauges as search efficiency, cost effectiveness, and total response time are interesting and useful for internal management and control purposes, but they should not so preoccupy the library that user benefits and satisfaction are assumed to exist. An active program of documenting specific benefits to the library's patrons is as important as keeping track of costs. Daniel Wilde presented one successful approach to this in the proceedings of the 1975 annual meeting of the American Society for Information Science.[1]

Among the minimal internal indexes that the manager of online reference services will want to compile for internal control and planning purposes are the volume and trends of searches performed; broken out, as appropriate, by user group, search site, data base, patron category, vendor system, time of day or day of the week, search category (standard or custom), individual searcher, and perhaps by other useful groupings.

Statistical summaries of this sort are compiled from the reports kept by the individual searchers. A typical searcher's time sheet and form used to collect accounting data are shown on the next pages. The cost and accounting data can then be used to calculate the average cost per search or per profile run (again, by categories if appropriate). The average cost per citation (or per relevant citation) selected or printed offline -- possibly by data base -- and similar figures, based on the fees paid by library patrons might also be revealing.

Another useful measure is the average staff time spent per search, ideally broken out into per-search, terminal time, and post-search activities. Much of this information has a bearing on the performance review process for individual in-

---

[1] Wilde, Daniel U., "Documenting User Benefits in An Information Analysis Center," Proceedings of the ASIS Annual Meeting, Vol. 12 (Washington, DC: ASIS, 1975), Part I, pp. 145-146.

TABLE 8-3: SEARCHER'S TIME SHEET

Please enter time in minutes to the nearest five minutes. Please date and initial each entry.

LIBRARY: _____

Patron name (optional): _____
Request number: _____

Originating Library _____

EVENT	TIME IN MINUTES	DATE	INITIALS
REFERENCE INTERVIEW initial patron contact			
ORIGINATING LIBRARY'S PREPARATION TIME without patron			
THIS LIBRARY'S PREPARATION TIME without patron			
COMPUTER CONNECT TIME	don't enter time (do date and initial)		
FOLLOW-UP TIME without patron			
ORIGINATING LIBRARY FOLLOW-UP TIME without patron			
FOLLOW-UP TIME with patron			
MISCELLANEOUS describe:			

CONNECT TIME	Patron present? Check if yes____	
DATA BASE	ELAPSED TIME	NO. OF OFF-LINE PRINTS

Use reverse to list additional bases searched on the same request as above.

TABLE 8-4: ACCOUNTING INFORMATION FORM

University of California, Los Angeles
405 Hilgard Avenue
Los Angeles, California 90024

Profile No. _____

            Date   Initials

Received _____

LAO _____

Date _____

Entered _____

Name _____

Telephone: Area Code _____ Number _____ Extension _____

Organization/Department _____

Address _____

City _____ State _____ Zip Code _____

Data Base Code (See Rate Schedule)	For current awareness service, enter period of subscription or no. of searches (e.g. 1 year; 6 searches)	For retrospective service, enter calendar year(s)	Amount in Dollars

Enter profile start-up fee where appropriate ($10) _____

TOTAL _____ $ _____

PAYMENT   Check ☐   Money Order ☐   Number _____

               Cash ☐   Purchase Order ☐   Number _____

                                       New P.O.   ☐

                                       Existing P.O. ☐

formation services librarians and supporting staff, but additional insights will have to be collected in this connection as well.

The facts on the causes, cures, and implications of operational problems must also be gathered and analyzed. Typically, many of these are brought out in regular staff debriefing sessions, such as those held monthly at the University of California at Berkeley. They include such matters as scheduling difficulties, search problems, system failures and interruptions, data base inaccuracies and faulty printout, errors or inefficiencies in search formulations, misunderstandings between patrons and library searchers or other staff, and problems between the online reference group and departments of the library or parent institution.

Meetings play a key role in communications between the coordinator or manager of the online reference services and the library staff. The minutes or summary reports of certain meetings can also be an important communications link, both within the library and between the library and its parent institution and other organizations. Other important media for management communications include formal announcements, reports, memoranda, articles, and the other written paraphernalia of administration.

Perhaps none, though, is of greater value than a basic manual describing the online reference services, setting forth their objectives and standards, and detailing the associated policies, forms, procedures, and organization. Developing such a manual, and keeping it up to date, should be an early and ongoing responsibility of the coordinator of the online services. The draft table of contents from the reference manual of Stanford University Libraries, which is shown on the next page, suggests one approach.

In preparing detailed procedures for the reference manual, the coordinator should anticipate and make provisions for problems and exceptions that might arise, so that they can be dealt with promptly and consistently. These exception routines are likely to range from the trivial (what to do if a patron neglects to pick up his search printout within a certain length of time), to those important enough to require a management policy decision (when a patron or searcher considers a search to be unsatisfactory, shall the search be rerun at no additional cost to the patron, or is a refund in order?)

Not every development can be anticipated, of course, nor should it be. A reference manual that attempts too much, quickly becomes unwieldy and defeats its own purpose. Properly done, however, it can be a very valuable resource for the information services librarians, as well as being the coordinator's single most valuable tool, both for communications and for the management and control of the library's online reference services.

TABLE 8-5: STANFORD UNIVERSITY COMPUTER
SEARCH SERVICES MANUAL
TABLE OF CONTENTS

Acknowledgements

1.0 ABOUT THIS MANUAL

1.1 Overview of Contents
1.2 Scope and Audience
1.3 Distribution and Revision

2.0 THE COMPUTER SEARCH SERVICE

2.1 Background and Objectives
2.2 Organization and Operation
    Chart 2-1: Computer Search Service Organization

3.0 POLICY STATEMENTS

3.1 Use and Access Policies
3.2 Service Policies
3.3 Payment Policies
3.4 Management Policies

4.0 PROCEDURES AND FORMS

4.1 Summary of How a Search is Handled
    Chart 4-1: Processing a Computer Search
4.2 Procedures
Procedure 01: Handling Initial Inquiries
Procedure 02: Accepting a Search Request
Procedure 03: Conducting a Search Interview
Procedure 04: Preparing Search Forms
Procedure 05: Formulating a Search
Procedure 06: Conducting a Terminal Search
Procedure 07: Preparing a Search Result Package
Procedure 08: Delivering Search Results
Procedure 09: Followup Evaluation
4.3 Potential Problems (In preparation)
4.4 Reporting Requirements

5.0 REFERENCE MATERIAL

5.1 Data Base Descriptions
5.2 Fee Schedule
5.3 Citation Explanations (sample only)
5.4 Sample Printout from each Data Base
5.5 Sample Publicity Items
5.6 Sample Completed Search Request Form

APPENDICES
A. Sample Blank Forms

Reprinted Courtest of Stanford University Libraries.

9
Conclusions and A Look at the Future

As online bibliographic services are instituted in libraries, the scene around the reference desk undergoes some remarkable changes. Without online facilities, the librarian has no choice but to turn to the traditional battery of printed abstracting and indexing services. With online facilities, the librarian has a very powerful alternative. The online version of the printed A&I files is usually superior to manual searching when (1) the search is complex, multidisciplinary, or must be pursued via more than one bibliographic resource; (2) the patron is interested primarily in recent literature; and (3) the patron can afford the cost of a customized service.

EFFECT ON PROFESSIONAL SELF-ESTEEM AND LIBRARY OPERATIONS

Online searching has provided a new dimension both to scholarly research and to reference library work. This "new" reference service is seen by some as a revolution in professional librarianship and by others merely as a natural extension of traditional reference service as it has developed over the past century.

Not the least impact of online services has been their dramatic enhancement of the prestige and self-esteem of librarians. Other impacts include:

- Increased staff workload;

- A surge in photocopying, interlibrary loans, and circulation to satisfy the demand for full-text documents;

- The need, nearly always, to charge patrons for online searches;

- The need to retrain and perhaps to reorganize the search specialists;

- The necessary investment in equipment and resources; and

The need to plan, control and manage these
new services.

Their advent significantly transforms library operations, alters patron service policies and collection development plans, and usually heightens patron impatience with slow delivery of the information items they seek once the reference citations are in hand.

EXTENT OF USE

The 1974-75 study sponsored by the National Science Founcation and conducted by Judith Wanger and others at System Development Corp. only reflected the first eruption of the volcano, or the tip of the iceberg, depending on whether you are hot or cold on the subject. In the three years since the study was completed, the number of libraries and other information service centers offering online services has probably doubled and redoubled. More than twice as many data bases are available for online searching now as there were in 1973. The number of searches conducted online annually is well over 1 million now and estimated to be growing by at least 20% per year.

An increasing number of users in scientific and technological fields have been served online during the past 10 years. Now humanists and social scientists can be served too. Faculty, staff, graduate students, and undergraduates are being served. Moreover, patrons of some public libraries have been able to take advantage of these services as well. Engineers, executives, lawyers, architects, and other professionals are also finding that some of their specialized information needs can be very effectively met online.

KEY QUESTIONS FOR THE FUTURE

This book has tried to reflect these developments. Among the key questions it has addressed are:

. What does all the activity in online services foretell for the future of library service? How will it affect the operations and services in a library?

The evidence to date indicates that these services will continue to have a profound effect, building traditional reference services into true, custom-tailored information services.

. Will online services deeply impact on collection development, interlibrary loan, photocopying, and circulation systems in libraries?

Emphatically so. Moreover, developments toward a national online bibliographic network bring added weight and pressure on libraries to make timely adjustments. The result should be the evolution of a total information service for users.

. Will more professional librarians be needed for these services or will the patrons ultimately be able to conduct their own online searches?

The odds are against the do-it-youselfer. Simple online searches, such as catalog checks for known items, may be done directly by the end user. However, the complex online searches discussed in this report are still too demanding to be conducted successfully by any but the trained specialist. There is ample opportunity for interested librarians to add online search skills to their repertoire.

. Might a coin-operated computer terminal next to the library coin-operated photocopying machine ultimately put reference librarians out of business?

Never. The introduction of information-retrieval technology simply enables skilled librarians to be more effective at what they have been doing all along -- providing professional service to those seeking information.

. Will online service ultimately replace printed A&I references?

Not likely. Each reference tool has its own uses. One can drive screws with a hammer but it is seldom advisable.

. Should a customized service be supplied by subject-matter specialists, or should reference librarians be specially trained to conduct online searches?

Both approaches are working successfully, in various kinds of libraries. However, a team effort, combining the patron's expertise with the search specialist's is the most popular approach, regardless of the search specialist's background.

What pricing policies should be established?

Many equitable and acceptable policies are in effect. Each library must set its own, in light of its circumstances.

• Can some costs be passed on directly to the patrons or to their departments or other organizational units?

The answer can or should be yes, in most instances, but obtaining such funds may be a new administrative problem in many libraries, especially public libraries.

These and many other questions can be heard whenever information professionals meet to discuss trends and developments in online bibliographic retrieval services. This is one topic that spans all types of library services for all types of clientele.

ROLE OF COMMERCIAL SERVICES

The systems design for online services does not rest in the libraries using them. Non-standard protocols and system features, access to data bases on several or only one system, charges by connect hour rather than for computer usage, and several other system-related factors are not under the control of the information services librarians. Librarians can and do exert some pressure for lower prices, more uniformity across systems, and improved access to data bases; but by and large, the problem of improving online services is out of their hands. Nevertheless, trends at commercially distributed online services must be closely followed by librarians. These commercial online retrieval services are creating profound changes in library management as well as in library service.

Another trend to watch is the move of fee-based services out of "free service" libraries into for-profit information companies, such as FIND/SVP (New York), Documentation Associates (Los Angeles), Editec and Searchline (Chicago), Information Unlimited (Berkeley), etc. These organizations have the ability to compete with libraries in offering computer searches, along with the delivery of full-text documents. To maintain their patronage in the light of such competition, libraries must find the financial wherewithal to provide fast, valuable services to an increasingly sophisticated and demanding clientele--either by charging patrons the full cost, or by allocating funds from elsewhere within the library budget.

A prime example of the commercial competition is Information Unlimited, of Berkeley, CA. Principals Sue Rugge and Georgia Finnigan find that they have been able to compete nicely with libraries, even though their fee for online searching is $50 per search plus out-of-pocket costs (i.e., connect time, communications, and printing). The average user spends $60-90 per search, with some paying $125 or more. Even students pay $30 plus costs. Rugge feels that their competitive edge is simply responsiveness. "Too many libraries take too long to respond to clients," she says. "We can get back to clients, results in hand, in half an hour." As some 80% of the firm's work is for corporations, the time element is apparently decisive. Information Unlimited also handles about 5000 requests for photocopies of cited material each month. Many of these documents are ferreted out for a client for whom the firm did not conduct an online search. The firm's network of full-text document hunters covers prime sources not only in the U.S. but as far afield as Japan and the Soviet Union.

Another firm that is successfully competing against large, university libraries that offer online searches at much lower cost is Documentation Associates (Los Angeles). Patricia Ferguson ticks off three major benefits that appeal to her clients. First, faster turnaround time. "Getting search results from a university can take a week or two," she notes, whereas DA can "rush things for a client in need."

DA's second selling point is quality. "Academic libraries often set aside a set amount of time for a search," according to Ferguson. "We take as much time as necessary to do the job right." The final selling point is "personalized service." Ferguson explains that "many people dislike dealing with a bureaucracy, and any library is a bureaucracy, especially the very large ones."

To be sure, most academic libraries are not interested in aggressively courting commercial accounts, but the success of information brokers like these, who use online searching when appropriate and charge enough to make a decent profit, has important implications for libraries of all kinds. Timely information has definite value which is recognized by realistic people in need of it. Fees -- even significant ones -- do not seem to be much of an obstacle to users who perceive the value.

CONCLUSION

Online bibliographic reference services have already made major inroads in government, special, and academic libraries, and are increasing their penetration of public libraries as well. Technological developments are lowering certain costs of providing such services, particularly computer and communications costs. The promotional efforts of both libraries and suppliers, combined with the word-of-mouth recommendation of satisfied users, seem destined to further widen the circle of users. The conclusion seems inevitable that online search services are here to stay. To everyone involved, they represent change and challenge. To some librarians and administrators they may be a demanding nuisance, or even a threat. But to a growing cadre of enthusiasts in libraries, they represent a distinct opportunity.

Selected Bibliography

Ahlgren, Alice, *Investigation of the Public Library as a Linking Agent to Major Scientific, Educational, Social and Environmental Data Bases.* Two-year Interim Report, Annex 1-Evaluation Results (Palo Alto, Lockheed Information Systems, 1976).

Benenfeld, A.R., et al. *NASIC at MIT*: Phase I report, 16 July 1973 and Final Report 1 March 1974.

Briggs, R. Bruce, "The User Interface for Bibliographic Search Services" in *The Use of Computers in Literature Searching and Related Reference Activities*, ed. by F. Wilfrid Lancaster (Urbana-Champaign: University of Illinois, 1976), pp. 56-77.

Charging for Computer-Based Reference Service, Proceedings of a Meeting, June 19, 1977, cosponsored by the American Library Association RASD Machine Assisted Reference Service Discussion Group and the RASD Information Retrieval Committee. (In press).

Christian, R.W., *The Electronic Library*: Bibliographic Data Bases 1975-76. (White Plains, N.Y.: Knowledge Industry Publications, 1975) 118 p. (Second ed. in preparation).

Collette, A.D. and J.A. Price, "A Cost/Benefit Evaluation of Online Interactive Bibliographic Searching in a Research and Engineering Organization" in *The Value of Information*, collected papers of the ASIS 1977 midyear meeting, Syracuse University, May 1977.

Cooper, Michael D. and Nancy DeWath, *The Cost of On-Line Bibliographic Searching*, technical paper, Applied Communication Research, Dec. 1976. (Also: Journal of Library Automation, 9:3, Sept. 1976).

Cooper, Noelle P., "Library Instruction at a University-Based Information Center: The Informative Interview," *RQ* 15:233-240 (Spring 1976).

DeGennaro, Richard, "Pay Libraries and User Charges" *Library Journal* 100:363-367 (February 15, 1975).

Elman, S.A., "Cost Comparison of Manual and On-Line Computerized Literature Searching," *Special Libraries* (January 1975), 12-18.

Ferguson, Douglas, "The Costs of Charging for Information Service" in *On-Line Bibliographic Services-Where We Are, Where We're Going* ed. by Peter G. Watson (Chicago: American Library Association, 1977) pp. 60-66.

----------------, "Marketing Online Services in the University" *Online* 1:3 15-23 (July 1977).

Hawkins, Donald, "Impact of On-Line Systems on Literature Searching Service" at 10th Middle Atlantic Regional Meeting, American Chemical Society, Philadelphia, 1976.

Hock, R.E., "Providing Access to Externally Available Bibliographic Data Bases in an Academic Library," *College and Research Libraries*, 30 (May 1975), 208-215.

Knapp, Sara D., "The Reference Interview in the Computer Based Setting," *RQ* Summer, 1978.

Landau, Robert, "ROBOT: An English Language Query Facility for Use with Data Management and Retrieval Systems" in *Proceedings of the ASIS Annual Meeting*, vol. 13, 1976.

Lawrence, B., B.H. Weil, and M.H. Graham, "Making On-line Search Available in an Industrial Research Environment," *JASIS* (Nov./Dec. 1974), 364-369.

Lipow, Anne G., "User Education and Publicity for On-line Services" in *On-Line Bibliographic Services - Where We Are, Where We're Going* ed. by Peter G. Watson (Chicago: American Library Association, 1977).

Lower Pioneer Valley Regional Commission, *Final Report, Regional Information System: Feasibility Report*, West Springfield, MA, 1973.

Maier, J., "The Scientist vs. Machine Search Services, We are the Missing Link," *Special Libraries* (April 1974), 180-188.

Maina, William E., "Undergraduate Use of Online Bibliographic Retrieval Services," *Online*, April 1977.

Martin, Jean K., "Impact of Computer-Based Literature Searching on Interlibrary Loan Activity," *Proceedings of the ASIS Annual Meeting*, vol. 14, 1977.

Pensyl, M.E., A.R. Benefeld, and R.R. Marcus, "The Techniques used to Promote Fee-for-service On-line Search Facility in a University Community," in *Proceedings of the ASIS Annual Meeting*, vol. 12, 1975.

Radwin, Mark S., "Choosing A Terminal," Parts I and II, *Online*, April, June, 1977.

Schwuchow, Werner, "Fundamental Aspects of the Financing of Information Centres" *Information Storage and Retrieval* 9:569-575 (December, 1973).

Stockey, Edward A., and Sandra J. Basens, *An Introduction to Data Base Searching, A Self-Instructional Manual* (Philadelphia: Drexel University, Graduate School of Library Science, 1977).

Summit, R.K. and O. Firschein, "Fee for On-Line Retrieval Services in a Public Library," in *Proceedings of the AsIS Annual Meeting*, vol. 12, 1975.

Wanger, Judith, Carlos A. Cuadra and M. Fishburn, *Impact of On-Line Retrieval Services: A Survey of Users 1974-1975*. (Santa Monica, CA: System Development Corporation, 1976).

Warden, C.L., *Online Searching of Bibliographic Data Bases, the Role of the Search Intermediary*, General Electric Technical Information Series Report no. 76CRD280. (Schenectady, NY: General Electric Corporate Research and Development, 1977).

Watson, Peter G., ed. *On-Line Bibliographic Search Services - Where We Are, Where We're Going*. (Chicago: American Library Association, 1977).

Wax, David M. *A Handbook for the Introduction of On-Line Bibliographic Search Services into Academic Libraries*. Office of University Library Management Studies, Occasional Papers, No. 4. (Washington, DC: Association of Research Libraries, 1976).

Wilde, Daniel U., "Documenting User Benefits in an Information Analysis Center" in *Proceedings of the ASIS Annual Meeting*, vol. 12, 1975.

Williams, Martha E., "Criteria for Evaluation and Selection of Data Bases and Data Base Services," *Special Libraries* 66:561:569 (December, 1975).

--------------------, ed., *Annual Review of Information Science and Technology*, various; annual, 1965- (White Plains, NY: Knowledge Industry Publications, Inc.).

Index

AGRICOLA, 37
ASIS (Amer. Soc. for Info. Sci.), 13, 110
Bell Labs, 19, 33, 58, 73, 87, 99
Bement, James, 41, 49
Bibliogr. Retrieval Svcs., 12, 35, 48
Brooks, Kris, 21, 47, 98
Budget, 29-31, 56, 59-62
Calspan, 93, 97, 99
Charles River Assoc., 32
Collection policies, 20
Collette, A.D., 62
Commercial services, 118-119
Computer terminals, 43, 44
Conclusions, 115-120
Cooper, M.D., 57
Coordinator (selection, duties), 101-104
Cornell, 20, 40
Costs, 9, 55, 57, 58, 117-118
Current Contents (Inst. for Sci. Info.), 37
Dallas Pub. Lib., 64, 73, 91
Dartmouth, 22, 74, 97
Data bases, selection, 37-39
Dalton, Edith, 40
Defense Documentation Ctr., 25
Dewath, N.A., 57
DIALIB, 14, 57
Documentation Assoc., 118, 119
Drexel U., 47, 50
Editec, 118
ENVIRON, 37
ERIC (Educational Resources Info. Ctr.), 4, 25, 57, 66
Exxon, 33, 62
Feasibility (prelim.) study, 27-29
Fees, 5, 22-23, 25, 26, 62-68, 115, 117-118
Ferguson, P., 119
Find/SVP, 118
Finnigan, G, 118
Graham, M.H., 98
Hawkins, Donald, 19, 99
Hitchingham, E., 107
Hock, Randolph, 49
Info. Unlimited, 118, 119
Interlibrary loan, 20, 115
Jaynes, Phyllis, 22
Knapp, Sara, 42, 62, 86
Lawrence, B., 98
Lockheed, 13, 35, 48
Lower Pioneer Valley Reg'l. Comm., 109
Management and evalu., 6, 7, 25-26, 101-114
Marketing and promo., 5, 23-24, 34-35, 89-100
Martin, Jean, 19
MEDLEARN (NLM), 47
MEDLINE/MEDLARS, 15, 57, 67
Messages from MARS, 50
Mich. State U., 103
Miller, Betty, 13, 93

Mindel, David, 13, 93
MIT, 39, 74
NASIC, 71
New York Times Info. Bank, 12, 29, 67, 91
Northwestern U., 29, 31
NTIS (Nat'l.Tech. Infor. Svc.), 25, 37
Oakland U., 107
Online Magazine, 50
On-Line Review, 50
Online services, advantages, 3-4
  costs and fees, 5
  extent, 3, 12-16
  future, 115-120
  impact on staff and administrators, 17-26
  intro. and overview, 1-11
  management and evalu., 101-114
  marketing and promotion, 5, 23, 24, 89-100
  modes of operation and svc. procedures, 72-88
  nature, 2-3
  organization, 39-40
  start-up considerations, 27-54
Oregon State U., 19, 21, 47, 56, 63, 74, 98, 99
Organization of online services, 39-40
Pearson, Ellen, 24, 86
Price, J.A., 62
Princeton, 77-78
Psych. Abstracts, 37, 66
Quake, Ronald P., 12
Radwin, Mark, 43
Redwood City Pub. Lib., 19, 41
Reference Services, 7
ROBOT, 10
Rosary College, 48
Ross, Ann, 46
Rugge S., 118, 119
Russell Research Ctr. (U.S. Dept of Agric.), 19
Sakai, Charlotte, 18
San Jose Public Library, 18
SDI (Selective dissemination of info.), 2
Searle, G.D., 46
Searchline, 118
Selection of online staff, 45
Self esteem (library staff), 22, 115
Simmons College, 48
Smithsonian, 25
Stanford U., 64, 74, 79-80, 113-114
SUNY (State U. of NY) at Albany, 62, 74, 75, 86, 91, 97
SUNY at Oswego, 56
Syracuse U., 21, 47, 50, 105, 106
System Dev. Corp., (SDC), 18, 21, 29, 48, 116
Training, 6, 45-54
Tymshare, 55
UCLA, 21, 47, 56, 73, 76, 81, 82, 112
U. of Arizona, 48
U. of Cal. at Berkeley, 39, 47, 93, 97, 102

U. of Cal. at Irvine, 83-85
U. of Cal., San Diego, 40, 65, 67, 70, 74
U. of Denver, 48, 50
U. of Guelph, 24, 86
U. of Illinois, 48
U. of Kentucky, 21, 43, 67, 74, 76, 87
U. of Minnesota, 94-96
U. of Nebraska, 29, 30
U. of Pennsylvania, 66, 87
U. of Pittsburgh, 50
U. of Rochester, 56, 102-103
U. of Toronto, 20, 24, 40, 48, 50, 74
U. of Washington, 50
Wanger survey, 13, 18, 20, 21, 47, 49. 57, 116
Warner Lambert/Parke Davis, 62, 86
Wax, David, 71
Weil, B.H., 98
Williams, Martha, 3, 12
Worcester (MA) Area Coop. Libr's., 40
Work load, 21
Xerox, 33, 41, 73